C000104371

NORMAL: A memoir of grief and healing

The events and
conversations in this book
have been set down to the
best of the author's ability.

Copyright © 2021 by Jade Price

All rights reserved. No part
of this book may be
reproduced or used in any
manner without written
permission of the copyright
owner except for the use of
quotations in a book
review. For more
information:
jade_price90@hotmail.co.uk

First Paperback edition November 2021

Book design by Canva®

ISBN 978-8-4910-9378-6 (Hardcover)
IBSN 979-8-7723-4106-3 (Paperback)

Acknowledgements:

This is for my Mama Bear. I am eternally grateful I was chosen to be yours. You taught me so many life lessons: one's I never even realised at the time. You are the perfect female role model I ever needed. You brought me into this world, and I took for granted, just how hard it would be to live in it without you. This book is to honour your story, my story and our story but mostly; this book is to honour you: all of you. I was given the privilege to have twenty five years of you; my repayment is to share you with everyone else. I love you more than yesterday but less than I'll ever be able to love you tomorrow.

To everyone who has helped and supported me through this journey, I will be forever grateful.

INTRODUCTION

I guess it makes sense for me to introduce myself, my journey and my story.

At the age of twenty five, life forced me on to a journey with grief. To say I wasn't ready would the biggest understatement of the century. I was just getting to grips with life itself, feeling like I was beginning to understand who I was and where I was going.

Grief is an unforgiving and destructive force; it's ugly, unashamed and completely brutal. It tears your life up and leaves the pieces flying around you whilst you're stood frozen on the spot. Not only are you experiencing the pain and the hurt of losing someone you love, you're involuntarily pushed into the ever-changing and confusing loss of yourself.

Anyone who has gone through it will relate to my experience and for anybody who hasn't, my journey will give you a window seat into its curse.

Eventually, each and every single one of us will experience and go through a journey with grief. Despite it being the one experience which unites millions of us, it's a journey that nobody can prepare you for. Everyone's excursion with it, is their own.

Nobody has a manual, it doesn't have a rule book to follow, there's no time table and there's no end date. Grief is a humbling and solitary experience. It's a shared experience worldwide yet painfully isolating.

At times you'll find yourself completely trapped inside its volt, and unable to shake free from its grip. Then there are the days where you feel in control and almost back to normal. A truly complex and confusing journey; with multiple bumps and stumbling blocks, yet a journey with absolutely no stop signs.

The clutches of grief's grasp never end, never stops and never releases you from its grip. You just start living again and its grip becomes normal. You become numb to its hold on you, numb enough to move forward but still conscious enough to never forget.

Whilst in the middle of my own journey, I watched a video about grief on social media and it explained it perfectly. In the video a psychologist drew a small circle, with a maze of lines inside. A similar circle was then drawn on the outside. They then explained that the bigger circle represents life and the smaller circle, with the maze of lines inside represents grief. Showing how grief possesses a significant space in our lives.

What resonated with me the most was when the psychologist drew another set of images on a new piece of paper. She drew the exact same maze of lines, but she drew a bigger circle around it. This time there was a greater distance in between the two circles. Then she explained that grief doesn't shrink, it doesn't just disappear and it doesn't go away with time. Instead what happens is over time, your life becomes bigger, and you begin to expand around the grief.

There has never been a more significant and simply perfect explanation to grief, than that video.

I've experienced a number of significant losses in my life. I have witnessed my maternal Nan's death with my own eyes; she died right in front of me. I've experienced the loss of each of my grandparents, both on my mother and father's side. I have experienced the loss of aunts, uncles and family friends.

With each experience, I was pulled into a false pretence of thinking I knew what grief was. I believed I knew what grief felt like. Each time I felt sadness, yet each time I managed to move forward and I did so very quickly. It never meant that I never loved them; it was simply due to my lack of life experience.

Every loss I've had was experienced at a very young age. I was too young to truly understand the gravity of what the loss meant, I didn't know what grief was. I was too young, and too naïve to understand the pain I felt and what it really meant. I had the beauty of childhood to protect me, so I never connected with the loss. I was able to understand that the person was never going to be alive again and I understood that they were dead. I just didn't comprehend what that truly meant, how that truly felt, and what consequence's it would have on life.

All that really changed with my experiences of loss was my age. The older I got, the more I understood the significance and magnitude of what grief really entailed.

I was faced with my biggest encounter with grief at twenty five years old. I experienced true grief and unavoidable pain. I was submerged into the deepest sea of sadness beyond imagination, and completely overwhelmed with pain on a daily basis.

I experienced, breathed and lived inside of grief. It was the most pain I have ever been in. It was real pain, not the kind that wears off in time. This pain was intolerable, it was suffocating and unapologetic. I couldn't escape it, each minute felt like an hour and the pain just seemed to intensify. I felt it physically, emotionally and mentally. My heart actually felt broken and I felt each sharp edge of the break inside my chest, with each breath I took.

My first real journey with grief tested me. Tested me beyond belief, beyond anything I could have ever expected or prepared for. It drove me fast into the darkest place I have ever been mentally.

It truly pushed me to the edge of life and I genuinely didn't think I would return. I was clinging onto life with every ounce of strength I had in me, but each day got more and more difficult: I nearly surrendered and let go. I believed I had nothing to live for and nothing to fight for. All of my happiness I once had; any happiness I was going to have was ripped away from me. I felt I would never regain the ability to feel happy again. If I'm honest, at the time, I didn't want to be happy ever again.

I felt isolated, suffocated, confused, numb, hurt, sad, guilty, angry, tired, sick, crushed, and empty. I felt every single emotion you can possibly think of, that doesn't involve happiness.

I'd never experienced ill mental health previously, until my journey with grief. I never believed that your mind could be broken, destroyed in fact. I never realised that your own thoughts could be your worst enemy.

Yet here I was contemplating with the idea of giving into these dark thoughts. Thoughts that were inside of my own mind, thoughts my own mind had generated and forcefully made me listen to. I never expected at the age of twenty five, I would be considering it being my last year on earth.

I was still so young. I hadn't even completed a fraction of the things I wanted to do. I had spent seventeen years in education; I had so many opportunities to find. I had so much life ahead of me, which needed to be lived, experienced and enjoyed. Yet here I was at twenty five, wanting nothing more to do with the life I now had: feeling like life had nothing left for me, that it had completely deceived me. It was cruel, unforgiving and completely sadistic.

I had lived life without any lesson of how to cope with grief. It was never a life lesson offered. Yet here I was, completely suffocated by that very lesson, with not one idea on how to handle it. I was completely out of my depth.

The worst thing is nothing can prepare you for it and despite now already having gone through it; I know that I will never be ready for it again. Even worse, eventually I *will* have to go through it again and more than likely, more times after.

I grew up with two incredibly loving parents, a mother and a father who shaped me into the person I am this very day. I'm the youngest of three, I have never wanted for anything; if my parents had it, they would have given me the world. More importantly, I was unconditionally loved and shown it daily.

I have been incredibly lucky to have the childhood I did. I've had a family structure for the entirety of my life. I've been witness to a relationship I could only ever wish for: my father worshipped the ground my mother walked on and equally she worshiped him too.

I took for granted each second of my normality. I didn't truly appreciate the surrounding love I had from both parents. I didn't truly appreciate the blessing I was given. If I knew at twenty five, the normality which I was accustomed to would be bulldozed, I would have never left my house. I would have taken a photograph every second of my life. I would have spent each second of the day with my parents.

If I would have known at twenty five, my life, my security and what I considered normal would be taken away from me on the 8th January 2016, I would have spent my life preparing for that moment. However, life doesn't give us that privilege and it's true, you never know what you have until you no longer have it.

Half way to fifty and I was dealt the worst hand of cards I could have ever imagined. On the 8th January 2016, my life shattered, time stood still, my heart froze and the breath in my lungs became ice.

On the 8th January, I became motherless. The woman I had grown up cherishing, admiring and unconditionally loving; was taken away from me without a second thought.

I wasn't ready and I wasn't prepared but life didn't care for that. It was her time to leave this world and leave me in it completely broken and destroyed.

The feeling of loss when it's your parent, your mother, is completely and utterly indescribable. Trying to explain or make sense of the feeling is impossible. People mean well when they say things that sound right and natural at the time, but their words have the opposite affect and cut you a fresh wound.

Some people don't even know what to say because they can't relate or understand your pain. I guess the only way I can try to explain the feeling of losing your mother is, imagine going to work, having a day with familiar faces, having a bad day or even a good day. Finishing work and then going home and having that desperate need to see your mother. To see her face, her smile, hear her voice, smell her perfume, hold her hand and cuddle into her body. Now imagine needing to do any of those things, but getting home and instead of her being there, all that hangs is a photograph of her on the wall because that's the closest you will get to her now and forever on. Now stop imagining and realise you can do all of those things, but for me; I don't have the option of imagination, I don't have the option to pretend, for me it's a dark, empty and heart-breaking reality, each and every single day.

Losing your mother is completely life destroying. Losing your mother as a young woman is soul shattering. Losing your mother as a daughter, who still needs her mum, is utterly heart-breaking.

To be that twenty five year old daughter, grieving the death of her mother is overwhelmingly painful, confusing and unfair.

The realisation that you'll have to fall in love; experience heart break, possibly get married, maybe birth a child and all other life altering experiences, without your mother, is when the loss becomes a complete reality.

Grief is a monster and it destroys your spirit, your soul and if you allow it, it will destroy your life. I went on its journey, hitting every single bump along the way, yet I'm here today and enjoying life once again.

I still feel uncontrollable pain and sadness, but the difference is I can now feel uncontrollable joy and happiness too. This journey doesn't have to end in despair and grief for others, this journey can be the making of you.

Join me, whilst I walk you through my journey. I hope this can bring peace and comfort to you. Knowing you're not alone and that everything you're feeling is completely and utterly justified and ok to feel.

More importantly, everything you're feeling, is completely and utterly normal.

CHAPTER ONE: Innocence of youth

I was born on the 20th December 1990, into the open arms of two strangers. Christine and Graham, but I prefer to call them mum and dad. I was set to be doted on, cared for and protected from this day forward. I would never go without, want for anything and more importantly, I would be given unconditional and undeniable love for the rest of my life.

My mum and dad were together for four years before I came into their lives. When they first met, dad was a twenty two year old manual labourer and mum was a thirty four year old; mother of two who worked multiple jobs. They both lived in the same area and circulated amongst the same friends. In fact, dad was actually dating a woman named Julie at the time (she later become one of mum's closest friends.)

Mum and dads' paths only crossed because dad's brother Mark was in a relationship with mum's friend Linda. Mum loved reminding dad that when they first met, she didn't particularly like him. Apparently, going as far as to say, and I quote: he made her skin crawl. It used to confuse me when she used to tell that story. I couldn't understand how they later got together, let alone have a child together, if she felt so repulsed by him.

One thing about mum, she isn't one to mince her words and certainly doesn't care how they land. Her view is, if someone doesn't like what she has to say or what she does, they don't have to listen or watch. A quality I really adore; the ability to truly have freedom over your authenticity and not be swallowed up or consumed by the judgement or opinions of others.

Curiosity got the better of me one day when I asked the question of how mum and dad got together. The answer I got wasn't the one I had anticipated for. I was expecting to hear how dad had changed his scruffy appearance, (again mum's words not mine) or how he organised some romantic and grand gesture to win her over. None of which were answers I was given. Instead the story of their big love affair goes as follows.

Mum had heard from idle gossip which was circulating, that she and dad were having this secret affair. Mainly driven from how much time they spent together through their mutual friends. Instead of rising above the childish gossip, mum decided that if people were going to talk, she would give them something real to talk about. Dad was invited over one evening and in mum's own words, he just never left, and as the saying goes, the rest was history. Not exactly the most morally focused plan, but it was a plan which would later create our future family. Which I'm guessing neither of them predicated would manifest.

There is quite a significant age gap between mum and dad, an age gap of twelve years to be precise. Being twelve years his senior, mum had herself a toy boy of which was a constant and on-going joke everyone liked to remind dad with. Despite the physical age gap, mentally and emotionally they were equal and had similar values and had both experienced a very similar up-bringing.

Coming from big families they were two of many children. Mum

was the eldest of her six siblings, made up of two sisters; Patsy and

Tracey and four brothers; Kevin, Steve, Malcom and Paul. Then dad

was one of ten children, made up of five sisters; Mary, Linda, Ross,

Susan and Jane and four brothers; John, David, Mark and Richard.

It's fair to say writing Christmas cards was always fun.

It wasn't only the size of their families they had in common.

Equally, both mum and dad were born into working class

households, where money was a struggle and life was lived to make

ends meet however possible. Sharing such similar circumstances, as

well as, equally having different experiences, (which today we

would classify as trauma) they both have the same fundamental

values that make up their personalities. They are both naturally

family orientated, with the ability to nurture as a second language.

They are both fiercely protective of their own and aren't afraid to

demonstrate it. More than anything, they both love hard.

With their values aligned, the age gap had no significant impact to their relationship. At the age of twenty two, dad had not only moved into a new relationship, he had literally moved in and began living with mum, but that wasn't the biggest life altering change dad decided to make.

Dad had come into mum's life when she was already raising not just one, but two children. Mum had two children from previous relationships; a twelve year old son Jason and a five year old daughter Kelly. Kelly's biological father being the only one to stay present in her life; so when dad decided to move in with mum, he also made a commitment to become a step-dad to both Jason and Kelly.

Unlike Kelly, Jason was old enough to understand what role dad was set to play in their life. Jason's biological father was never present and in fact Jason doesn't know who he is. For many years of his childhood, Jason was raised by Kelly's father; an experience that probably stalled his acceptance to dad.

Jason witnessed how ugly things can get. The relationship between Kelly's father and mum wasn't healthy; actually that's a massive insult to the reality. Mum had spent many years being mentally, physically and emotionally abused and Jason witnessed all of it. All the pain, the hurt and the bruises: he witnessed how a man, who should have been playing a father figure to him, was hurting his mum instead.

The birth of his daughter didn't put an end to the abuse, he continued and so did mums endurance to it. Until one day when she did thankfully, find the strength and courage to break free from her prisoned relationship. Having a father who threatened to show him how a real man fights, made sure he left mum alone. Thankfully I have never experienced what it's like, to grow up witnessing an abusive relationship. To think about the amount of pain and abuse that man caused and inflicted on my mother makes me physically sick. I am certain that people can change and I hope that, those who have the opportunity to change do so, but as contradicting as this is; I whole heartedly will never forgive the actions which; granted I never witnessed myself, but actions I know my mother suffered from.

However like I said, she did find the strength she needed to break away from that relationship and from the moment she did, she decided that she would no longer be anybody else's punch bag. Mum would no longer accept anything less than the respect and appreciation she deserved. The re-building of her life gave her the inner-strength she carried into the rest of her life. It is exactly the same strength I adore and admire today.

To say dad was facing a challenge and an uphill battle, would be the biggest injustice to what he faced. Walking into Jason's life after he had already seen how bad it can get, Jason made it his mission to make dad's life a living misery. He stole and sold all of dad's jewellery; he broke his things and constantly reminded him that he wasn't his real father. Regardless what was thrown at him, dad took it and dealt with it. Not only that, he was proving Jason's internal issues all wrong because he stayed, and he never retaliated. He stayed because he loved mum and equally she loved him just as much.

Dad treated her like a queen and he made sure that he showed her how much she was truly worth. He helped piece back together all of her broken shards and restored her faith in real love. They became each other's equal, it was a partnership and whatever one of them had, they both shared. The true reality is; if anyone was in charge in their relationship, it was mum; she most definitely wore the trousers. Dad's 6 ft. and stocky build was no match for mum's 5 ft. and plump statue. Apparently you have to kiss many frogs to find your prince, but mum never found hers. Instead she found herself a king.

I don't really know all the minor details of the big love affair that was mum and dad, but what I do know, it was already written in the stars. Mum loved to get her fortune told and receive readings. I've been told many stories of her visits, and despite not personally being the biggest fan of the art, this particular fortune telling story is one of my favourites.

Mum had a favourite teller who she would go to called Iris. This one particular reading she went to, Iris told her that she would meet a tall, dark haired gentleman (I know how original) and that he would be the love of her life and together they would have a baby, a blonde baby girl. Mum was also told that this man would hurt himself in an accident on a bridge. Thankfully the third prediction has never come true.

If you believe in the world of fortune telling; it's fair to say dad was already in the wings for mum. He was mum's tall, dark haired gentleman (thanks to his Native American roots) and you guessed it right, I was the blonde baby girl. Whether or not that makes you want to go and book a reading, or if you think it's just a pure coincidence, or complete horse shit, mum's fortune this time round came true.

It was four years after dad had come into mum's life, that our family became the complete package it is today. At the age of twenty six, dad became a father and at the age of thirty eight, mum gave birth to her third child: only five days before Christmas. When most families were getting prepped for Christmas day, mum and dad were nursing new born: whilst still working out the existing family logistics.

Dad had now become a father to a new born, but he was still learning the ropes of being a dad to a nine year old girl and a now sixteen year old teenage boy too. Kelly was now old enough to understand the step-dad situation. Following on in Jason's footsteps, she tried her hardest to sabotage the relationship. Exactly like Jason, she would break dad's belongings and was just an outright little terror. Yet once again, nothing worked, dad still stayed and was resilient to any attempt to make him leave.

The one aspect Jason and Kelly failed to consider was how much, mum loved dad, and how much she knew she had found the one. For her, she had completed her family, a family she wanted to raise with the man she loved. Mum knew what was happening, so she laid down the law. Telling them both if they were trying to make her choose, they wouldn't like the outcome. Weirdly, from that day forward they both stopped trying everything they could to get dad to leave.

When mum laid down the law, there was no alternative but to listen. For a woman whose natural facial features ooze warmth and kindness, within seconds she could make your blood run cold. Her small brown eyes would draw you in and her thin lips were always shaped into a smile, she possessed the aura of a mother, yet when she meant business she would have you wishing for another mother. At times it was hard to take her too serious, especially with her rounded cheeks and neatly permed hair, but it was never too difficult to snap out of it. As soon as her eyes seemingly changed from brown to black, you knew that was it.

Eventually Kelly and Jason gave into the situation and accepted that dad was for keeps, and indeed, wasn't going anywhere. Then fast forward to today, he isn't considered or thought of as anything other than our dad. He isn't a step-dad to anyone, he is simply dad, and in fact he's also a granddad now too. (Nine times over.)

I was privileged to grow up living with both of my parents. It shaped my understanding of what a family structure was and how it should look. My parents remained together throughout my childhood, and I believed this to be normal. I soon realised however, what I perceived as a normal family structure, wasn't the same for everyone. Many of my friends had parents who were separated, and so obviously their perception of what a family structure looked like was completely different to mine.

I actually really struggled to grasp the idea that other kids my age, didn't live with both of their parents. Instead they would live with just one and then visit the other regularly, normally on weekends. It totally intrigued me when friends told me they were going to their dad's for the weekend. It completely obliterated my conception of what a family was.

The most obscure aspect for me; believe it or not, was when the step-parent card was thrown down. Logically I simply couldn't quite get it. I couldn't process that, someone had another parent, who wasn't actually their biological parent. Now of course, let me address the elephant in the room (or on the page). I am fully aware how strange it is for me to say that, after explaining my own family set up. My dad was literally, exactly what I was confused most about… he was himself, a step-parent.

When I was struggling to process the family dynamics of others, I actually had no idea the reality of my own. I was living with my mum, dad and my sister at the time. My sister never called our dad by his real name; I only saw or heard my dad be referred to as dad. None of us were treated any different, we were all his kids. So I grew up with the understanding that the very man I called dad, was also the same man my brother and sister called dad too. I never knew he wasn't in fact, their biological father.

Therefore, learning that other kids my age literally had two separate families was an alien idea and concept to me. Neither my brother nor my sister would go to their fathers for the weekend, and like I said, the only person they called dad was the same man I did, so I really never knew any different. Of course, there was the day where I discovered that dad wasn't Kelly and Jason's biological father.

It was a day that caused my brain a great deal of stress; especially being so young and having so much innocence in my understanding of life. It was a day where my brain nearly exploded. Hearing the actual reality of things was so confusing and completely surreal, it was a real challenge for me to try and accept.

To discover that, what you believed to be your normality for so many years, actually had an alternative version of truth, was overwhelming. I remember freaking out, thinking my family was falling apart and that my brother and sister weren't my real brother and sister. I genuinely thought this was the end of our family, I even considered the idea my dad not actually being *my* real dad. All these complicated and world shattering thoughts sent my poor innocent brain into a semi melt down.

After the initial shock and devastation at the thought my family was going to leave me; absolutely nothing changed. Everything I was witness to, my family, our bond and our structure stayed the same. My dad was still referred to as dad by all three of us and before I knew it, this massive revelation was very easily and quickly forgotten.

I guess all that changed was the normality. What I once understood to be normal to me was no longer true. I had another version of normal, and very quickly, I'd adjusted to it. My family structure still remained; but the foundations had slightly changed. It definitely taught me a lesson: you shouldn't judge others because you can easily become the one who is judged. However now, way past the age of innocence, the lesson I have taken from this part of my life is much more profound.

It was a lesson in normality, with a clear message that what I may find normal doesn't mean that it is. Every single one of us has a perception of what normal is and each of our 'normal' can and does, frequently change. Normal is not a definite or solid state, it's completely ambiguous and fluid, so how can something that forever changes be defined?

One aspect of our family that did change was, Kelly and Jason now had a younger sibling. I was (and still am) referred to as the spoilt brat. Anyone who is the baby of the family will more than likely have the same stigma. Obviously from my point of view, I of course am not a brat, nor am I spoilt. The truth of the matter was; I was born at a time where the circumstances of our family were different. When I came along, there were two parents who were both bringing in an income, granted an income that didn't mean we were rich, but there was definitely much more disposable income.

All three of our childhoods had different circumstances, but none of us went without. If mum and dad could afford to give any of us something we wanted, they would. It's also very important for me to stress that, as soon as I was old enough to earn my own money, I got a job and soon started to pay for what I needed and wanted from my own pocket. Regardless, I am still the family brat.

There's a nine year age gap between me and Kelly, and a sixteen year age gap between me and Jason. As they're both considerably older than me (sorry I had to), they already had their own things going on. Kelly had her own friends to hang around with and Jason was hardly ever around. He was somewhere, doing something, mainly causing mischief. We did see him every now and then, but he mainly did his own thing.

Jason soon got into a serious relationship with a girl who lived next door, called Sam. This only made the time we did see him even less. I remember, even when he was at home, he would always find a way to be next door with Sam. His typical trick and method was to climb out from his bedroom window, across and into Sam's window. How he never broke a bone, is beyond me.

Although Jason was hardly around, Kelly was, but having your little sister pestering you and your friends, wasn't considered cool. Apparently I 'cramped her style;' of course this never stopped me trying. We had a very typical older and younger sibling relationship; in fact this one particular memory really sums up our relationship.

I decided I would clean her room one day, whilst she was out. My mum refused to go in there to clean it, my sister never decided to do it either, so it was a shit tip to be perfectly honest. With Mr Muscle in hand I took off upstairs. I started with my own room first, before moving onto the actual hazard.

Mum came up to inspect my room, which resulted in great feedback. So after mum went back down stairs, I moved onto my sister's room. Due to the fact I wasn't allowed in there, I had to keep my decision to clean it a secret. It was going to be a surprise for her. However, little did I know the actual surprise was for me! When I opened the door, I froze from what my eyes witnessed, it was disgusting: I hadn't realised just how much of a task it was going to be.

For the next hour or more, I cleaned my sister's room. It took the soul out of me, even at the age of say nine or ten, I was no older than that; I struggled with energy. I polished every inch of that room, including furnishings that didn't need it.

Next I moved across to putting the pile of washing away, which was lying across the floor. Washing that later turned out to be, not the clean pile I thought it was. As soon as I opened the wardrobe doors, instant regret hit me in the face, along with every single item of clothing my sister owned. For a good half an hour, I sat amongst the floor-drobe; I folded each item of clothing my sister owned, (mostly unwashed) neatly enough for the wardrobe doors to shut.

After I finished being Cinderella, I was so happy with myself that I needed to show mum. So off I trotted downstairs to tell her my about my good deed. However, all I got in return was being told not to go into my sister's room, "it's her mess and she should do it", oh and of course, to "stay out" of her room once again. It wasn't exactly the response I was hoping for. Maybe my sister would be more thankful; after all, I did do her a massive favour.

When she came in, I dragged her upstairs, opened her door and told her to look inside. She took one step inside; swings around and tells me through gritted teeth, not to go in her room, and not to touch her things. Instantly my face dropped from the absolute lack of appreciation and rudeness.

From that moment forward, I never went into her room again: well, apart from needing to borrow a CD or anything else I felt benefited me more than her of course.

To be perfectly honest, majority of the time I was a loner and spent a lot of time in my own room, making my own fun and entertainment. If I wasn't in my room playing in my own world, I would spend most of my time around adults, mainly with mum, dad and their friends. It's probably fair to say a lot of the things that I found fun and considered entertaining, was not so fun and entertaining for other kids my age. I loved helping mum clean and I would always have my dolly in tow, of which I really considered to be my actual child. What I really loved more than anything though, was helping dad in the garden, either maintaining it, building things or even better, breaking things.

I was very much a tom boy growing up, and to still to this day, I'm still pretty shocking at being a girl (I still have no idea how to walk in heels or where contour goes). I just prefer building, fixing and breaking things more than I do playing with make-up and getting my nails done. My enjoyment for all things tom-boyish allowed me to spend loads of time with dad, which is probably why I am such a daddy's girl.

Anyone can tell you how much we both adore each other. I am the complete apple of his eye and equally he is mine. He has always tried to be the best dad he could be and still to this very day he tries ridiculously hard. I just haven't got around to telling him he doesn't have to try so hard, he's a natural. We've always had an incredibly strong bond, he's not only my dad: he really is my best friend. He's my favourite human in the world to be perfectly honest.

Dad taught me to ride my first bike, how to fish and he helped me with every piece of homework I had. I am his pride and joy and he's never failed to show me how much he loves me. Not only is he proud, he is incredibly protective: some may even go as far as to say over protective.

As a baby; I had a problem with my eyes which saw me having to go into hospital. What made my condition even worse was the fact dad never let me cry. If he could do anything to stop me being upset he would. The nurse told dad that if I wasn't allowed to cry, my tear ducts wouldn't develop correctly. This led to a verbal fight with the nurse and resulted in dad having to leave the ward: he wasn't best pleased with the idea of letting me cry.

I'm sure my Aunt Tracey would agree that dad is overprotective. When she would look after me, she was given a strict time schedule to have me back by. All because dad didn't like me gone for too long and not know how I was.

Even the nursery staff would have probably agreed too at, how over the top he was. They had little to no choice but to watch, whilst I was carried away, crying in dad's arms, all because I wanted to go back home. Despite them insisting it was completely normal and that all kids get upset: especially on their first day, dad explained I wasn't 'all kids' and that my first day at nursery, was also going to be my last day.

A lot of people would probably say I have dad exactly where I need him, and I guess to some extent it's true. The one parent I didn't have wrapped around my fingers though, was my mother. It never mattered how much I cried or screamed, I was never going to get my own way with her. Mum was much tougher to work; she was definitely the stricter one. There was only so far you could push your luck before she gave you the death stare. Even today that look would make my knees buckle. It must be a mother thing: she was psychic I swear. It never mattered how big the wall was in front of me, she would just know exactly what face I was pulling behind it after being told off. That used to freak me out so much.

CHAPTER TWO: Innocence of youth part II

Although mum was definitely the stricter parent, it was through her parenting where majority of our morals and beliefs stem from. Mum was very traditional and old fashioned, she was brought up with the view children should be seen and not heard.

Mum's own childhood wasn't exactly the easiest. As the eldest of her siblings she joined ranks with my nan and helped to raise her brothers and sisters. My grandad had an unhealthy relationship with alcohol and the law. Her, my aunts and uncles didn't have the best upbringing, it was tough but they were unconditionally loved. They'd lived the best they could in the circumstances they'd had. Of course it was a completely different time back then and most of their neighbours and friends were living in the same conditions too.

Mum's childhood did mean that she was forced to grow up quickly and mature quicker than her age. Whilst some kids were playing mum to a dolly, she was actually playing the role of parent to her brothers and sisters.

All of this conditioned her into the mother she was to us kids. As I said, she was the one who planted and enforced our morals and beliefs, some of which we still have to this very day. I compare my behaviour and attitudes from when I was a kid to kids growing up today. I can see the differences and it's quite striking, how different it is. I know that if I ever spoke to anyone the way I hear kids speak today, I would most definitely see the back of my mother's hand, or slipper. I don't even want to know what the consequences would have been if I spoke to her the way I hear some kids speak to their parents today.

Mum was really big on respecting your elders; this was probably her main rule for all of us. I grew up referring to all my elders as aunts and uncles, regardless if there wasn't a single strand of D.N.A connecting us. Everyone was auntie or uncle; from actual family members, distant relatives all the way to just family friends and neighbours. I was taught that it was a sign of respect and it was good manners. Even to this very day, I will refer to most of my elders as aunts and uncles.

The problem with having so many aunts and uncles around you; it gave you no hiding spaces or any room to be a little git. If I did anything remotely against the rules or anything that would lead to the probability of me getting into trouble, it would indeed, just lead me to the 'getting in trouble' part. It was like mum and dad had their own personal spies dotted all around. Anything I did wrong, mum and dad would know about it before I even stepped back through the front door. It honestly made playing knock down ginger a bloody nightmare.

I don't think there was ever a time I did get into trouble. Kelly and Jason not only call me the spoilt brat but I am also the goody too shoes to them; simply because I have never wanted to do anything, remotely wrong or particular risky enough to land me in trouble. Even as an adult I'm the same. I'd rather not take the risk of getting into trouble if I don't need to.

It has nothing to do with wanting to be the good person, or being the person who always does the right thing. For me, it comes down to me hating the idea of disappointing anyone. The thought of having to apologise or explain myself, and someone being disappointed, makes me feel sick with anxiety. The idea of having to lie to somebody too, makes me uncomfortable. Obviously we all tell those little white lies, even me, but it makes me feel really uncomfortable. I prefer to tell the truth regardless how hard it can be.

I thrive when people around me are smiling, laughing and genuinely happy. I am a people pleaser and I will try to do anything I can to make sure someone is happy. To know I have disappointed anyone honestly makes me feel awful, so for that reason I always try to do the right thing.

I guess it always helped having a dad that is overprotective. I would need to tell him exactly where I was going; who I was hanging around with and what time I would be home. Add all of that together with, the amount of aunts and uncles I had dotted around and the fear of my mother's death stare, getting into trouble was practically pointless and simply not worth the hassle.

The only thing I ever did as a kid; which you could class as being remotely rebellious, was riding around on other people's bikes. Although this may not sound 'rebellious,' the issue was, I would go on a search around my estate for bikes which had been just left outside. When I would find one, I'd take it and ride around until I was bored and then return it to its rightful owner. Even my small act of rebellion and theft still ended up with me doing the right thing.

Despite that story also sounding really sad and as though; I never had friends and just rode around on other peoples bikes everyday all by myself, I was actually quite happy with that. I would actively choose to do my own thing; I've always enjoyed my own company. I found myself getting really bored of games or the pointless and continuous wandering around in a group. My idea of fun was creating things, but doing it on my own.

I remember being no older than eight years of age, and my idea of having a fun weekend was setting up my very own business; a street market sale.

I had set up tables which dad helped with, again a very supportive father. Once I had everything set up and ready, I took all the items from my room I no longer wanted and I priced them up and put them up for sale for passing strangers. My sales patter must have been really great, because I very rarely had anything left by the end of my shift.

I do have to admit though, not all the items sold were always 'unwanted' or 'unused.' If I am going to be perfectly honest, the prices which I put up didn't always return a profit either.

One particular weekend, I had opened up shop outside our house: as normal the tables were filled with all my items, ready to be snapped up by the passing strangers. Now because I was a little girl, I like many others had a dolly and a pram. My pram was amazing, it was a '90's multi-coloured' 'all the works chid-carrier' and I absolutely loved it.

I decided as a responsible doll parent, that I would bring it to what I considered, 'work.' I parked the pram up next to my table, and began my eight year old working day. The trade was going well; I was selling items left, right and centre. Then this old lady approached and what happened next, demonstrates the exact reason I shouldn't, and will not, have real children.

The lady asked me how much I was selling the dolly and pram for; now remember, these weren't up for sale. I had simply just brought along my doll child to work with me, in fact, I hadn't even had them for long: they'd been given as a Christmas present.

I looked at the lady, looked back at the pram and my dolly sitting inside and without a second thought, or a slight hesitation, I told the lady it was a total of two pence. I explained that it would be one penny for the pram and another penny for the dolly. Just like that I had sold my doll child with pram for two pence. How I have never made it into business I don't know, how much more cut throat can you get?

Although I was delighted I had another sell out day, mum and dad was less than impressed. After all, I had literally sold my Christmas present that probably cost several pounds, for just two pence. They probably would have been less annoyed if I had auctioned myself off.

I however, soon ran out of things to sell to the general public. I'm surprised I even had a bed left to be honest, and after pram-gate, mum and dad were very reluctant to buy me new things: weird if you ask me. The business woman in me though, and the addiction of sales was too strong to ignore.

I decided on a new venture. I handmade tons of these friendship bracelets from string, and started to sell these to the general public instead. I switched up my strategy this time though; instead of sitting outside my front garden, I situated myself at the corner of my road. The 'child me' had such a cunning mind-set. I chose the corner because it leads onto the main path towards the local shop. A pure genius decision if you were to ask me.

I would like to take this opportunity to apologise to anyone who ever bought one of these bracelets. I am pretty confident that they were a complete pile of rubbish. However, they did sell like hot cakes and I'd learnt my lesson from pram-gate too. I'd increased my prices, and sold each one for twenty pence; granted I still probably only earned enough to buy more string. I'm sure mum and dad were pleased when I got older and my love for entrepreneurism declined, I mean, who knows what I would have sold if I had continued.

It wasn't just as a child where I tried to avoid getting into trouble though. Even as a teenager I avoided all possible trouble too. I never got into a fight; in fact I never even had an argument with anyone. I never did the whole 'telling your parents you were at a friend's house' when actually you and your friends were getting off your face with the cheapest vodka in a field. Instead, I would be sat at home with my parents, again not because of them, but because I chose to and if I had the chance to go back, I would make that same choice each time.

I simply wasn't interested in being rebellious or getting myself into trouble. The thought of having to explain the reason I'd lied to mum and dad and waiting for their disappointment, filled me with inner fear. I had a good enough relationship with the pair of them, where I could have openly told them that I was off to a field with my friends, but the reality is, it just never really interested me anyway. I preferred to be at home, spending time with mum and dad and being in my own space. When I am at home, I am around my creature comforts and I can do what I want, when I want and how I want, without having to worry if someone else is having fun.

I'm fortunate with the relationship I have with my parents. We've always had a strong and close relationship, they've continuously given me the best support, guidance and respect I could have possibly needed. I know that not everybody has the fondest memories of their childhood or of their parents and that breaks my heart. I can't imagine not having the feeling of warmth when thinking about my childhood and for that, I'm eternally grateful to mum and dad for creating that experience.

When looking back I never had all the latest fads or the on-trend brands, I was even the last one in my friend group to get the internet, and I was fifteen. We didn't go on lavish and expensive holidays aboard, all of those things are just materialistic and what we didn't have we simply made up with time. We spent time together and we did things together.

One of my favourite things to do was to go to work with mum, because for hours it would be just us two spending time together. Mum worked at a workman's club as a cleaner in the mornings, doing three to four hours a day and then worked in a laundrette in the evenings. Of course I was never allowed to go to the laundrette, but I did love going to the club of a morning with mum.

We would walk through the graveyard on our way there and talk about how beautiful the flowers and headstones were. The minute we got to work, we would sit down and have a cup of tea first, that was very important. Mum's best friend Aunt Pat also worked there, and each morning, before they started work, they would always have a cup of tea, a cigarette (back when you could smoke inside) and a good gossip. I loved this part of the day because I got to have snacks from behind the bar and a drink (obviously a soft one).

Mum would arm me with polish and a cloth and let me loose on the tables and beer trays. I was in my element: I loved every second. There was one room in the club that had a stage and a massive wooden dance floor; and this is where I would put on a quick show for mum and Aunt Pat. They would be in stitches, more than likely because I was rubbish and had no talent at all.

One thing mum let me do which I absolutely loved was to check under all the chairs and tables for change. Mum told me that when people sit down sometimes pound coins would fall out and they never noticed. Whatever I found I was allowed to keep and buy whatever I wanted with it. You can only imagine how precise I was when I was looking for this money (I was more thorough than a crime scene investigator).

I only went to work with mum on the weekends; because obliviously I had school every other day. After me and mum were finished with work, dad would meet us and together we would walk into town and do our weekly shopping. Normally we would stop and get a café breakfast and then mum would drag us around to every single charity shop she could. Searching and looking for new cardigans, flip flops, and not to mention, books. She'd had an obsession with incredibly sad and disturbing books. They would, without fail make her upset, but she couldn't get enough of them. Her favourite was A Boy Called It.

My memories are not filled with things I never had or what I never owned, my memories are filled with all of the times we spent and did things together. Memories for me are built on experiences of time, not things we own or have and when it's all said and done, the memories we will all reflect on in the end will not involve any materialistic possessions.

Although we didn't travel abroad on holiday as a family, we still had family holidays, but they were in the UK. Each year we would go down to Devon and have a week long caravan holiday. We absolutely loved it. Me, Kelly, mum and dad would go together with my Aunt Pat, Uncle Mol and their daughter Caroline. Aunt Pat and mum were inseparable and as a result, Kelly and Caroline became best friends too.

Each year Kelly and Caroline tried their hardest to get out of coming with us, they wanted to stay at home; but neither of them could have been trusted to do that, they were better under supervision. All I have from these holidays are happy memories, ones that still make me laugh, which is all we did, we spent most of our days in hysterics.

There's one specific year that's a highlight for all of us. All for the completely wrong reasons, but so wrong they turned out right. Our annual holiday to Devon had come around and we'd decided to go to a place called, Ilfracombe. Now before I reminisce about the holiday, I would like to state that Ilfracombe is a beautiful place and somewhere I would happily go back to, but our first experience would not have resulted in a glowing trip advisor review.

This year we chose to stay in a maisonette, instead of our usual caravan preference. That was our first struggle. When we'd arrived, we'd been told where our maisonette was located and then given the keys, so far nothing out of the ordinary. We found our maisonette and attempted to unlock the door, which wouldn't budge. They had accidently given us the wrong set of keys; so instead of being regular human beings with brain cells and going back to the front desk, we believed it would make more sense to, try and climb through the window that was open.

From the outset, the holiday was going to be one to remember for sure. Every single morning we would be woken by the loudest sheep I have ever known to live. It was also the week where I'd learned to swim, and it didn't happen with the fondest of memories either.

All week we would go to the communal swimming pool. Dad, Kelly and Caroline would normally play around in the outdoor pool, which was basically as deep as the ocean. As I couldn't go in that pool, dad would take me to the indoor pool and for hours, try to teach me to swim. It's important to mention now that, my mother absolutely hated water. The hatred was that bad, her baths would never be higher than her belly button, in the fear she may drown. So for her to watch me every day in the pool, learning to swim was torture.

For the whole time dad was trying to teach me to swim, I had to wear arm bands to keep me afloat. I was getting quite good at it and was quickly getting the hang of it; before I knew it I was doing laps of the indoor pool. However, this one day, I was so excited, I wanted everyone to watch and witness how well I was doing, completely ignoring the fact that I was still having to rely on arm bands.

Everyone apart from mum and I were around the outdoor pool, so I ran round to get everyone. I was so eager to show off; I continued to run back to the indoor pool, unable to wait for everyone to follow. As I was running around the pool, trying to get my arm bands on ready for my big performance, I slipped and fell straight into the water. It was in that moment that I really learnt how to swim.

All I could hear was my poor, panicked mother screaming for my dad. I laugh at it now, but back then it was very traumatic. Thankfully, I managed to stay above the surface and dad was in the water way before I could be in any real danger. From that day forward, mum wouldn't let me back in the pool without my armbands. She would refuse to come and watch, it left her completely traumatised.

All our holidays, now looking back, actually contain real milestones in my childhood. I learnt to swim and of course nearly drowned in the process, but one other memory that really stands out, is finding my first real love.

This discovery came when we went on a caravan holiday to Dawlish. We would routinely go down to the onsite club house in the evenings. They would put on entertainment for the kids and then whilst the adults enjoyed a comedy show or a game of bingo, us kids would be taken to the kid's only area. It was in that kid's only area where I met my childhood sweetheart. Unfortunately, despite the love we had, his name has literally no place in my memory, so for the sake of details, we will call him Dawlish boy.

We would chase each other around, meet at the swimming bars and in the evenings we would play air hockey. I remember one evening we were watching Casper the friendly ghost, in the kid's area and that's when Dawlish boy asked me to be his girlfriend. The next day I told everyone I had a boyfriend; mum and Aunt Pat were so happy and asked all about my little Dawlish boy. Dad on the other hand was less than impressed. Just like all good love stories, there was to be a small heartbreak; which came in the form of the realisation I was going home and wouldn't see Dawlish boy again.

Mum and Aunt Pat sat me down and asked if I wanted to write him a letter and give him something to remember me by. So that's exactly what I did. I wrote Dawlish boy a little letter, telling him how much I would miss him and mum told me to put our address at the bottom so he could write back. Now are you ready to hear what I left him as a present to remember me by? I left him a full size; probably around four foot tall, silver inflatable alien. I know, so bloody romantic.

All I needed to do now was to give him the letter and his present, so Aunt Pat walked me round to find his caravan. When we found it, we realised that nobody was in, so creepily we stuffed the alien and letter through the kitchen window that was left open. (I wish I could have seen the reactions to a suddenly present inflatable alien in their kitchen.)

I did receive a reply from Dawlish boy; he even sent a small passport photo of himself with his letter. That was his present for me to remember him by, which I guess made so much more sense than a life sized blown up alien. Unfortunately, our relationship sizzled out and we stopped writing to each other, the big holiday romance was over and strangely I carried on living my life.

It's only as we grow older, that we can truly appreciate those moments of pure innocence. Times where we didn't have many concerns or worries and where we never really felt heartbreak. Where things were much simpler and pure, all of this changes of course, when we go into adult life. We no longer have the privilege of being naïve and innocent. When we're faced with a problem or a situation that requires action, we don't have the protection of being too young anymore. As adults, we're forced to handle life in its entirety, for all of its goodness and certainly for all of its ugliness.

The day I faced the reality of no longer having the innocence of youth on my side, was when I heard two very simple words. These two words shook my entire world and echoed in my ears for days. Those two little words were non-Hodgkin's lymphoma.

Chapter Three – A Virgo VS Cancer

Non-Hodgkin's lymphoma… within that split second, a doctor gave

mum the diagnosis we all feared but didn't believe would come true.

Time stood still and silence fell over us like a sheet of deafness. The

only word, I processed was Cancer. Like a choir of screams,

chanting the word over and over and over again. Each time; hearing

it louder, seeing it bigger, feeling it harder, tasting it sourer and

smelling it fouler.

It is truly such a confusing state of mind. All five senses being

simultaneously pummelled, yet every sense you have is equally

numb and non-respondent.

All of this started with a simple but persistent cough. With mum

being a smoker, having a twenty a day habit for over fifteen years;

we simply put it down to the cigarettes. Together with the cough,

mum had noticed a small lump. It was the size of a golf ball on the

side of her neck. We all assumed it was due to the constant coughing

she had done for weeks. However with the push from Aunt Pat, mum

decided to make a doctor's appointment to be safe.

The doctor told mum that he didn't think it was anything to worry about. Still he referred her to the hospital for a biopsy, again to be on the safe side. He also told her that, the smoking wouldn't help, and to try cutting down.

Even the doctor believed it was nothing to worry about. So why would we have been worried?

Although I can't say for sure, whether or not it had crossed mum's mind but it never for a second crossed my mind, that it could be the big bad C word.

Mum's appointment for the results had arrived and I went to the hospital with her. Sitting in that waiting room felt like an eternity. Have you ever looked at a clock, saw the time, looked back to see the hands have only moved two minutes; yet you could have sworn you checked the time an hour ago?

I could almost hear the batteries in the clock drain with energy. All I could do was watch mum. I kept glancing at her face witnessing her mind pondering, getting lost in the anticipation of expectation.

I could tell mum was nervous and was panicking, understandably. I didn't let her know that at this point, so was I. However, it still didn't cross my mind something serious was happening.

'Miss Wilkins?'

For some reason my gut told me to go into the room with her. Now, this may not sound as weird to other people but mum was a woman who did things by herself. She would have normally told me no and to be perfectly honest, I was expecting her reply to be just that.

'Yes, come in with me.' These words had butterflies fighting the lining of my stomach. Now I knew… mum was worried.

As we both sat down in the room, mum faced the doctor and I sat to the right of him. Looking back it felt almost like an interview. It all happened incredibly quickly.

-Being called into the room.

-Sitting down.

-Getting the diagnosis.

-To leaving with our world flipped upside down.

I hate using the phrase; 'you don't know how it feels, until it happens to you.' However, experiencing the destruction of what that disease does, the moment you are faced with the knowledge you, or a loved one, has got cancer, you truly can't understand the brutal winding that information does.

It really knocks the wind from your soul and it shakes you to your core.

It pounds you in every way, shape and form. It attacks you; physically, mentally and emotionally.

Within seconds, each thought turns to panic and heartbreak.

Automatically, without meaning to, you think the worse and remember all of the horror stories you been told about the monster that is cancer.

The doctor gently dropped the bombshell:

'Miss Wilkins. I am really sorry, but it is cancer.'

Mum's face dropped and in that second I knew that nothing she was about to be told, would register or even be heard. I mean, in that moment, I could barely breathe and think at the same time, so I can't imagine what she was feeling.

Her face was masked with sadness and emptiness.

It was now all on me.

I had to be responsible for listening to what the doctor had to say.

Almost a role reversal, I had to be the protector, the comforter and the responsible adult.

What the hell was happening? Why did my heart feel like it was beating inside my throat? Why did my head feel like it was vibrating in an ocean of water?

A situation no child should have to witness. The moment the woman who gave birth to you, wiped away tears and nursed you when you was sick, adapts a childlike state of mind. Yet, a situation that comes more natural than imaginable. All that mattered was, I loved her and I knew she was unwell so naturally; protecting, comforting and taking responsibility over shadowed any conception of normality. The woman who was naturally designed to nurture, was now in the polar opposite condition and was wrapped under my nurturing cloak. I had to remove myself from my emotions and channel my concentration correctly. I took one final glance at mum.

I had to do this, my shoulders increasing in weight, from the pressure of the situation.

Mum was completely zoned out; spiritually, she was no longer present.

It really felt that someone hit the slow motion setting on life's remote control.

It felt like that moment lasted for a decade, not only was we stuck in slow motion, we were experiencing an outer body as well.

You feel like a witness to your own life and everything is just happening around you but at the same time without you. All of your interpretations of reality trapped, under this new sense of insecurity and forced acceptance of change.

After a deep breath, I asked the doctor to tell me the facts, was my mum going to be ok?

If I'm being honest, I didn't care for the facts and stupid long medical terminology. All I could hear was my inner voice cry; *is she going to be ok?*

Is she going to die?

As a heads up to any medical professionals; none of us have a clue what you mean when you use, the long proper terms you've been taught in medical school. Regardless how tough it will be to take or to handle, don't beat around the bush: just say it.

Say it in all its ugliness because if it's bad news, you're not going to be able to protect anyone with words. Especially words no one understands.

"It's Non-Hodgkin lymphoma, it's an uncommon form of cancer and it affects the lymphatic system which attacks the lymph nodes all across the body."

He continued, and told me that mum's cancer had been detected at a very early stage and that this was a good thing. The chance of survival was very high.

Despite the doctor being seemingly confident in mum's chances, I still had to be told in the most basic terms.

Will she die? That was what I needed to know. Probably not the subtlest way of asking but it was the only thing I cared to know in that moment.

"Without treatment, yes this can be fatal. However, as we've caught mum's early, we can cure this and the chance of it returning is low. Your mum will be ok."

That was it. That was my hope and all I needed and wanted to hear. My mind held on to that sentence. 'We can cure this' this was my only interest. Mum was going to fight this even if she didn't want to; together we were going to do this. If she couldn't, then I would.

Time had completely thrown us under its hypnosis. Ten minutes felt like an hour. Transporting us from the present and placing us in the future. The only problem is I would have preferred to have gone back to the past. We were under times control and it was manipulating our conception of its format.

Once we had seen the doctor; to my oblivion, there was a nurse who was standing in the room with us the whole time. She escorted me and mum to the family room.

The family room was a strange place if I'm totally honest.

It was a cramped back room with a light baby blue leather sofa, which felt like ice to sit on. On the left to the sofa was an ice blue arm chair to match. A coffee table with gossip magazines spread across the surface (I didn't quite understand that commodity.) On the other side of the room sat an old fashioned reading chair, probably pulled from the waiting room. It seemed to have been stripped of all human contact and stood uninvitingly alone. The walls were all painted white, abruptly reminding you of the clinical space you were in.

The atmosphere felt suffocating and overwhelming. It was spaciously cramped. Words echoed through the stillness of the room, bouncing off the cold walls, avoiding any connection to the people engulfed inside its core.

The room in fact, was a far cry away from the intended family feel its name suggested.

The nurse placed a box of tissues on the table, giving the subtle permission to let go of our emotions. Mum did just that. She completely let go and it was devastating. My heart broke once more in that moment. Crumbling inside, piece by piece sinking to the pit of my empty stomach.

Although I felt emotional and distraught, physically I just couldn't cry. I wanted to, almost desperately needed to, but I couldn't.

I think because mum was so upset, subconsciously I couldn't let her know I felt helpless. She had been told she has cancer. Regardless how broken I felt, she needed to know that her support network would be her strength, not a crumbling mess.

I couldn't even tell you what the nurse said or what the room was intended for. Possibly designed for clarity and composure? I didn't know? What I did know however, was that once again time had manipulated our sense of its format, making minutes feel like hours. On the departure of the family room, the nurse gave us some leaflets and a number for McMillan that we could call at any time if we had questions or needed someone to talk to.

That moment right there was the most affirming reality check. That was when it finally hit me, the reality of what my mum was facing and going up against, hit me like a tonne of bricks.

The moment my five foot nothing, mouth all mighty and loveable mother was going head to head with the most evil killer known to living things.

All sense of our normality had been shredded and pieced together in a different order.

Mum's friend Jim, picked us up from the hospital. That journey was completely surreal and one that will never leave my memory. A familiar face, a journey back home and music on the radio, it was an utter head fuck to be honest.

We had been given news that changed our world as we knew it and everything felt different. Yet now, we were back into the normality we had before we were given the news. It was like we had witnessed a scene from the future and then had to go back to the present. It was all very, very surreal.

We got close to home and I asked if mum wanted to go straight home or if she wanted to go to her friend Linda's.

I knew she needed to have a good cry and needed someone she could talk openly with. There were feelings she had, that I knew she didn't want me to be aware of. Despite me seeing the fear and uncertainty in her face, she just couldn't say them to me. You see, my mother had strong traits of the Virgo, she didn't really know how to ask for help, even when she needed it the most.

As we pulled up at Linda's house, I told mum that I was going to go home and wait for dad. She asked if I was sure, but I knew she felt relieved I was going home and that she now had the opportunity to have felt her true feelings. Before I turned to go home, I gave her a cuddle and a kiss on the forehead, which was when she asked me not to tell anyone yet.

The walk home from Linda's is a five minute walk at best, and it was another out-of-body experience. I felt completely and utterly suffocated. My auto-pilot kicked in and my feet took me home. My thoughts were racing in the freedom of my head.

If it wasn't so rooted in my head as to where I was going; I think I probably would still be walking to this day.

I finally had that silence, that air, that space and that alone time to process the last hour or so. It was both smothering, yet completely liberating at the same time. A real perplexing head space, I had so much freedom to run into but I had no-where to go and was trapped. I got to my front door and inhaled as deep as I could and as I have ever done before. As I opened the door my sister was in the living room hoovering.

Don't tell anyone yet… don't tell anyone yet… don't tell anyone yet

This span around my conscious mind, stuck on repeat only to be broken by my sister's request for information.

"How did she get on?"

"*Don't tell…* It's not good news, she has cancer but she will be ok. She's at Lin and Mark's."

FUUUUUUCK… my inner voice screamed.

I had told someone… I had one job, just one job but it slipped out.

Literally the words spewed from my lips, not even touching the walls of my mouth on the way out.

What else was I supposed to say? I had to tell her. So that was the "don't tell anyone yet" out of the window.

With that my sister put the hoover away and said she was going to see mum.

"Kelly, mum doesn't want anyone knowing yet. Please don't go telling anyone just go straight to Lin's."

I know, what a hypocrite.

In all blunt and selfish honesty, I was so relieved that Kelly wanted to go and see mum because I needed to be alone and to finally process my emotions.

As the front door closed, silence fell over me again and now I was truly alone. It was finally just me, my thoughts, my feelings and my space.

I went into the bathroom, pulled the toilet seat down and took a seat. The emotions I had harboured for the past few hours were finally free. I unleashed all the tears, the fear, the panic and the sadness.

For some reason, I have always felt at peace and tranquil in the bathroom. I don't specifically know why. I could spend hours in the bath and do nothing, not even think, just be and simply exist. So in that space, I felt safe, I felt truly overwhelmed yet at the same time strangely calm.

I'm not too sure of time specifics to be honest: in fact, I could swear that day had more than twenty four hours in it. However dad finally came in from work.

If someone had told me all the clocks in the world had stopped, I would have believed them because that's exactly how it felt.

All I knew was, I was no longer crying and I had to come out of the toilet. Dad asked straight away how mum got on.

This was now getting harder to follow mum's instructions of not telling anyone yet. Low and behold, it came out. Once again the words flew between my lips without hitting the walls of my mouth. "It's cancer, it's called Non Hodgkin-lymphoma, the doctor said it is treatable and that she will be ok."

Like father like daughter, dad was faced with the worst diagnosis but remained calm and didn't flinch.

In fact, dad had a bath. Needless to say we both find solace in our own company (and the bathroom clearly.) When he got out, he walked up to meet mum to walk her home. Even if he wanted to burst out in hysterics, he wouldn't do that, not in front of me anyway and vice versa.

I couldn't tell you how long mum was out for or what time it was specifically her and dad came back home. Of course they returned. I couldn't tell you what we did, or what we spoke about for the rest of the day. All I do remember was speaking about telling the rest of the family.

As an incredibly stubborn woman, again true to her Virgo traits, mum originally didn't want to tell anyone. She said if it wasn't for the fact I went with her and heard what the doctor said, she wouldn't have told us. Enter the most commonly used phrase ever: 'everything happens for a reason.'

Right then and there, my reason to go into the room smacked me harder than the word cancer itself. I went into that room so that mum wouldn't have tried to face this alone. Thank the universe.

It was a battle trying to persuade mum that telling her brothers and sisters was the right thing to do. The one question she couldn't ignore and I think eventually, was the reason she told everyone, was how she would feel if one of them kept something like this from her. Yes of course she had the right to not tell anyone, of course she did, but to play devil's advocate, we as her family, also had the right to know. We needed to be prepared for the worst and not have a nasty and fatal surprise one day.

We all came to the final decision that she would tell the rest of our family.

After finishing her cup of tea, (I'm sure if you cut her open, her blood would run a constant stream of PG tips,) we then began the horrific door knocking and life altering bomb dropping. It felt like we were a really crap delivery service if I'm honest.

It's in these devastating situations; you truly see the beauty of humanity. People regardless of age, gender, beliefs, class or wealth, all feel pain the same way. It doesn't discriminate, irrespective of who we are, pain hurts. It's what changes you from just a human being to being a person. Human beings are what science defines us as, but people are what unite us.

When something hurts so much that it shoots that pain from your gut, all the way to the heart, we all become the same species. We become people again. Caring, affectionate, vulnerable and compassionate, we become alive again and not just another number in existence.

Granted there will always be different reasons behind pain. The fact remains, pain is pain and it's a feeling we are all going to at some point feel.

I believe now more than ever that there is no such thing as blood is thicker than water. Instead, I believe that love is stronger than labels. It doesn't matter if you're someone's mother, daughter, husband, partner, friend or even dog for that matter. When somebody is loved, that's the only thing that defines the relationship, not the status.

We all know somebody who doesn't get along with a family member, and has a strong relationship with a friend. They probably class their friend more as family than the family member they don't get on with.

Now that's simply because love has nothing to do with DNA or blood.

I watched so many people in my mum's life get told that she has cancer. Her brothers, her sisters, her partner, her children and her friends, and at no point did anyone take the news better or worse than another.

All of us took the news the same. We all took it painfully.

Not one of us was affected more because of who she was to us, or what relationship label we had to her. We all felt the same pain, due to the love that was present for her.

The most common comparison in society I guess is a celebrity death. Let's take Whitney Houston for example.

I would happily guess in a ratio setting, there were actually more people that grieved her death who didn't know her personally, compared to the people who were personally affiliated to her.

This is not to say that, those who knew her personally didn't grieve more or less than anyone else. It's an example to show that regardless of relationship labels, when somebody is loved, blood and water become irrelevant and love becomes the strongest bond over any label.

For a few days after mum told her nearest and dearest of her diagnosis, people would come and see her to make sure she was ok. People would check to see if she needed anything and to offer their apologies.

That's the funniest thing about us human beings. We feel so many complex and crippling emotions, none of us really know how to deal with them or even really how to express them. None of us know what the right thing to say is.

We all know how we feel and what we think, and we all understand our own emotions. We can all comprehend them in our own minds, but we all struggle putting them into words for others to understand. "I'm so sorry to hear," is the worst right thing to say.

It doesn't even make sense. What are you sorry for? What have you done? Why are you sorry to hear?

To offer an apology to someone is to excuse yourself from a mistake or a bad decision you have made. So, why on earth are people sorry when someone receives bad news?

What have they done wrong? Has anything they've done, contributed or played a vital role in mum having cancer? No not at all, of course not. Yet for days this was the most over used phrase I heard.

At the time I didn't understand why people kept saying it and it got to the point I would get angry when I heard it.

Yet I know for a fact I am completely guilty of saying this when I hear bad news about someone. The reason why? It's simple I think. As people we feel empathy and I genuinely believe the true meaning behind I'm so sorry, is the feeling of not being able to help but to have empathy in abundance.

It's our polite way as people to say: I feel so sorry for you. Of course now I see it, but the next person that said that phrase, would have gotten a punch.

As much as she dreaded the whole situation; having to break the news to her family and friends, I think the response and reactions she got, massively helped her. I know for a fact it confirmed to me who cancer had decided to have a fight with.

We were an army ready for battle, each one of us. This was one fight cancer wasn't going to win.

In the commencing months, mum had various hospital appointments and consultant meetings. The most important one was the plan of action for treatment and what the battle plan was going to be.

It was set to be a mixture of radiotherapy and chemotherapy.

Looking back now and witnessing what both these treatments entail, I struggle to see the therapy aspect of both.

The side-affects and the destruction to a person's physical appearance, is a complete contradiction to the definition of the word therapy. However, I guess when weighing up the pro's and con's, the pro's completely top trump any cons of the treatment.

For majority of mum's life, she was a plump and full figured lady.

When she became poorly, she shrunk to a tiny frame and for those that knew her for years, noticed the stark contrast in her appearance.

This only grew more noticeable when she started her treatment.

<u>Chapter Four– The Fight Starts</u>

The fight was on and in absolute truthfulness, mum took an almighty battering.

Although she would never admit how tough it was, you could just tell. Her moods were completely erratic and at times she was a different person. All of which were understandable of course, she was after-all fighting cancer. Despite having the sympathy of every one of us and the understanding to her short temper.

As a family, we spend most of our time annoying and aggravating each other. Therefore, we all treated mum exactly how anyone should be treated, normally. We treated her no different to how we did before the cancer diagnosis.

If she was being horrible and too miserable, we would tell her exactly that. We made no excuses and no exceptions.

The cancer wasn't going to take anything away from her, wasn't taking her spirit, her laughter, her attitude, and it most definitely wasn't going to *take her away*.

When she felt like she couldn't make a cup of tea, she was made to make that cup of tea. If she was grumpy, she was made to snap out of it. We all did our fair share in wearing body armour to take the abuse, but she knew it would be fired back. So really for her it wasn't worth it. Wait until you hear some of what we did.

One afternoon she came back from her first radio therapy session with a photograph of what can only be described as the best Halloween mask I have ever, ever seen.

A white plastic netted mask, covering the line of the shoulders, face and head. The mask is completely tailored and shaped to the face, which made it look even more frightening. It was basically a plastic version of mum just with no features.

Each radio therapy session comprised of mum having to lie down on a table, with the mask placed over her face and then fixed to the table. Obviously, this is to ensure you are kept still during the treatment.

I can't even begin to imagine the fear that it creates. It's an unnatural situation to be in, your body practically being shackled to a table, yet your mind drowning in freedom and running a marathon of thoughts.

Forgive me but I am unsure whether mum's radio and chemo treatment ran simultaneously or separately. To be honest I can't even remember which one was first.

I never experienced what the radiotherapy sessions were like, Kelly or dad would normally go with her when she had these sessions. I do however remember the chemo side of the treatment.

I went along with mum for a few sessions of chemo. I'll do my best to walk you through the process as I remember it.

I believe mum's appointment was an early afternoon slot. I don't particularly remember the day; let's just call it a Monday for now (no-one likes Monday's.)

Her treatment was held at Medway Maritime Hospital, which to be honest, has a pretty poor trip adviser review.

Before I go into the whole process of what mum went through; I would like to stress, the McMillan cancer department at Medway hospital is an incredible asset to our health service. One in which, I would never ever say a bitter word about. It's incredibly underfunded but run by priceless souls.

Now back to mums treatment.

We arrived at Medway hospital, found our way to the chemo ward, mum was then booked in and we were shown to her treatment chair. Neither of us were aware how long this treatment would take, so being comfortable was going to be a must. I'd be lying, if I said I wasn't relieved to see the chair mum was given, assuming that I would also be in a similar one.

I was very wrong to assume. I quickly discovered what I had to sit in: for five hours, may I add. To try and describe this chair would do an injustice as to how uncomfortable it was.

I understand that may be the most insensitive and self-absorbed comment to ever be made in consideration of the event. However, for anyone who has ever accompanied someone whilst they have chemotherapy, you will know how relatable this comment actually is.

Just to be clear, I would absolutely, without hesitation and in a heartbeat, sit in that chair for 72 hours again if I needed to. I am trying to lighten up what was actually one of the toughest days I've had the displeasure of experiencing.

So, mum is now comfortable in her chair, blood's taken, blood pressure checked and all other pre-observations done. She was now ready for her treatment.

I couldn't help but scan the room and look at the other patients who mum was sharing this horrific and intrusive experience with. I was brought up not to stare as it's rude, but in that situation I simply couldn't help it. My heart sunk and continued to sink each time I laid eyes on someone else in that room.

In some respects, it was a glimpse into what our lives were to become accustomed to. There were patients who were at the end of their programme and were having their last session. Patients who were half way through the programme and then there were patients, who were at the beginning of their treatment. A complete time line of sadness, worry and hope.

Each time I unintentionally scanned the room, my eyes would re-divert to mum and I just couldn't help but feel uncontrollably sad.

I wouldn't describe the feeling as pity. I didn't have pity for anyone in that room. Not because I am a heartless cow but, because each person in that room, was a fighter. All of them showed strength that you just cannot pity. The feeling's I had, and still to this current day have, are empathy, respect and utter admiration.

I remember looking at one lady in particular and she had already lost all of her hair. Granted I can't actually be fully confident that, it was a result of the treatment. However, given the circumstances, I think it's safe to assume that was exactly the reasoning for her hair loss. To me, although it was a sharp image to take in, I didn't know this lady. I had no image of her before treatment; my experience of her was that she had no hair. I knew no different, this was how she looked. I however, have a different normality with my mum, she has always, to me, had hair.

I didn't realise in that moment that I was fixated on the other patients, until mum hit my arm to stop me from staring. When mum caught my attention, I was pummelled with an instant bolt of emotion and dread.

I grew up with mum having the thickest head of hair, always neatly brushed and styled. I was now faced with the reality that, the image of the woman I had growing up, was going to dramatically change. Cancer was really giving us its showreel and we got to see what its capabilities were. In that split second, reality really hit home and it hit super hard. This was actually happening. My mum has cancer. I think that moment was the first time I truly accepted reality and the realisation that my normality had once again changed.

In all chemotherapy sessions, the patient has to have a line put in so that the drugs can be infused into their blood stream. There are a few different approaches to this; a line can either be inserted into someone's upper arm, their hand or into their chest.

Mum's line was inserted into her upper arm. After the line was inserted, the nurse propped mum's arm up with a pillow so that she was comfortable. Next was adjusting the seat, now for those who know mum, it will come to no surprise that she wanted the chair in full recline. I mean why not, this was definitely the time to be Mariah Carey and diva the hell out of people.

Connected to mum's line was a fluid bag of drugs raised by a drip stand. The stand itself had this blue box with an orange LED screen, to which detailed how long the infusion would take.

I want to make you aware of this blue box, as every patient had one and when the battery was low or when their infusion hit specific times, the box would scream an alarm.

Now I would like you to imagine a room of six maybe seven people all hooked up on their drip stands, all having different timed infusions, all having the alarm function.

After the first, let's say ten minutes, it was easy to cope with and block out. Now after the first hour, this box has become my nemesis. If I concentrate hard enough, I can still bloody hear that thing in this present day.

So mums all hooked up and ready to be infused. I look at the blue box, which for now was a dream and hadn't made a sound.

I saw thirty minutes on her screen. I was dumbfounded, this incredible therapy that kills and attacks the most evil, venomous and destructive disease known to mankind, only took, thirty minutes (cue the moment my discovery was abruptly shattered.)

"Don't get too comfy mother, you're done in half an hour." This was met with absolute hysterics by the nurse. Finally someone finds me funny, except, I didn't say anything humorous.

Still laughing, in fact almost holding back tears of laughter, the nurse kindly clarified, that mums' box was set for 'every thirty minutes' and she was due two rounds of fluid. She informed us that were going to be there for a few hours at least.

Jokes on me, that bastard box will go off every half hour for the next few hours. This was the moment, where I discovered I would be sat in the worlds' most uncomfortable chair for hours, five hours, to be more precise.

What was the lesson that I learned from that day? I learnt to hide my emotions and expressions of course, as I think my face said it all. As the nurse finished telling us of our expected wait time, her and mum looked at me and just hysterically laughed. I couldn't help but join in, mainly due to confusion.

Regardless of what or why; hearing and seeing my mum laugh in that moment, was soothing and priceless. It made the situation so much more bearable and it lifted that uncomfortable cloud that we found ourselves under.

My heart felt so full and heavy. I really felt her laughter, it wasn't the feeling of a normal emotion it felt physical. That little snippet of her happiness wrapped its arms around my heartache.

The day seemed to last an eternity. Those who accompany somebody going through their treatment, ensure that you have something with you to pacify the time. Something I leaned quickly and made sure I did going forward.

After a while, I could see fatigue cover mums face. It's a typical symptom of treatment and in fact many of the ladies and gents around us were having small snoozes. Mum however, fought the tiredness and really held onto her consciousness. I think it was a mixture of anxiety and uncertainty; it wasn't exactly every day you found yourself in that situation.

The ward facilitated our dietary requirements and supplied some lunch. Endless supply of tea and coffee too, which was heaven sent. This was mainly to help with peoples blood sugars etc. I don't really understand the full science behind it so I'm not even going to attempt to explain the how's and why's.

The time eventually ticked on and honestly, removing any emotional attachment, the process was incredibly boring and clinical.

We did have the radio playing in the background, which suppressed a small percentage of boredom. All in all though, it was draining and there were only so many times you could read a sign detailing how to wash your hands, before you started to see illusions of the words dancing on the paper.

Mum was finished and the time flipped from a.m. to p.m. after hours of treatment. Before they let you go home, they carry out basic observations, like blood pressure etc. By this point mum looked exhausted. I just wanted to get her home and tucked up in her own comforts.

We were finally en route home and mum really fought the urge to close her eyes. Her tiredness was so visible, I could almost hear it. I didn't think that having treatment, which on the surface didn't seem too heavy, would wipe someone's energy out so much.

As soon as we stepped through the front door, I helped mum take her coat off and then she fell onto the sofa. Her exhausted body was cradled by the cushions and I don't believe I've seen someone look that comfortable in my life. Snug as a bug would be an understatement.

Prior to mum being diagnosed with the big C, one of her on-going health issues was her circulation. Her hands were always mauve and she had not one ounce of heat circulating through them. Her hands and feet were always as cold as ice.

Now my poor father and I on the other hand, let's say we're both blessed with a body for an arctic winter. So I'm sure you can appreciate that when the fire and heating was on at the same time, we both really struggled, mainly with heatstroke and dehydration.

Back to the story, when we returned from mum's treatment, the fire was already burning and chucking out heat from hell. Yet mum's jaw was still chattering away, from being her usual cold self, so I flicked the kettle on and brought the big guns out: mum's hot water bottle.

I plonked the hot water bottle down (her eyes lighting up with warmth) and put her tea on the table, she was finally home and comfortable, my brave, strong and incredibly tired Mama Bear. Within a matter of minutes she was out for the count, and was snoring her face off.

Her mouth was wide open, the hot water bottle was wielded to her grip and her tea was getting cold. She looked at peace so I laid a blanket over her and just watched her as she slept. It was then and there I felt the tiredness and exhaustion within myself.

I sat down with dad and we comfortably sat in silence. Our new reality surrounded us, whilst our new normality settled in. I remember looking at the TV for ages but at no point was I watching it. I couldn't even tell you what was on. I do remember zoning back into the room and glancing over to mum. If I am completely honest, I felt overwhelmed and utter helpless.

Nothing is more excruciating than watching someone going through something, which they've not asked for and having to watch them become so fragile and vulnerable but not being able to help. Of course we were all there for her, full support and love; but as invaluable as that is, you still feel completely useless. You want to help fight away the pain, the exhaustion and make it all go away, but you can't. All you can do is stand witness.

Mum's treatment lasted for months; she had chemo every two or three weeks. Again, my memory of all of the small details are sparse I apologise. I think if I'm being warts and all, some of these details have been so far suppressed they've actually been erased (exactly what you want when writing a book!)

What I do remember is mum's hair started to become increasingly thinner. Each time she washed and brushed it, the strands of hair soon became clumps that fell out. I remember one morning she was really upset, because it was the first time she had woken up and saw her hair on the pillow.

By this time she had already completed at least three rounds of chemotherapy and hair loss was only one of the symptoms and side-affects she faced.

Her appetite had also declined and her dinner portions became smaller and smaller. She had developed small mouth ulcers too, which didn't help as they caused discomfort and pain every time she ate. As her appetite declined so did her frame, she became incredibly frail and she had lost a considerable amount of weight. I believe at one point she weighed no more than eight stone.

Her dramatic change in physical appearance was a real challenge to accept. The woman I grew up with had completely changed. Cancer was truly throwing some almighty punches and they seemed to land, each and every time. Despite the brutality mum was facing she wasn't going down.

One afternoon I had come home from work and mum was having a bath. At this point, mum was so frail and weak that she had to be helped in and out of the bath. For a woman of independence and pride, this was absolutely humiliating and frustrating for her. None of us were fazed by helping her and we never at any point saw this for anything less than it was. To each of us this was natural and normal, but mum absolutely hated it.

While mum was in the bath she asked me to wash her hair for her. In this moment it was more evident than ever, that her hair was rapidly vanishing. The way my hands simply fell through her hair onto her scalp was devastating. Each time I massaged and lathered her head in shampoo, I would have a palm full of her hair. It seemed to be just oozing out of her scalp.

With each massage, my heart obliterated further. I wanted to cry with each movement I made. I think mum had sensed my sadness and asked me "is it a lot now?" I wanted nothing more than to deny any acknowledgment of what was happening. I wanted more than anything to be able to say no: that she wasn't losing her hair but what would that achieve?

Lying to her when she knew full well what was happening, would not have helped. After all, she was sitting in a bath with clumps of her own hair swimming around her.

All I managed to respond was "quite a bit." The words choked me and my throat burned with pain. I couldn't say anything else, because I would have filled the bath up with my tears. Instead I blinked away my tears and started to rinse the shampoo out, resisting touching her hair any more than I needed to. It didn't help though, it was still oozing out and I felt like I was just washing it out of her head.

I sat with her until dad came in and got her out the bath, which thankfully, wasn't long. The image of my frail mother, sitting in the bath surrounded by her hair, broke my heart into pieces. When dad helped her out of the bath, she practically ran to the fire to dry off, (you guessed it, she was cold.) After finally warming up a little she went back to the bathroom and put on her pyjamas.

After a while, she shouted for me, so I did no more and went to see what it was that she wanted. When I went into the bathroom I was frozen on the spot, I wasn't expecting what I saw.

Mum was just standing there with dad's hair clippers in hand and simply asked if I was ready.

I remember checking if she was sure, she of course replied in her typical fashion, and I quote, "I'm losing the fucking thing anyway." So there I was, standing in front of mum who was holding a pair of hair clippers, waiting for me to shave her head bald. I don't think mum actually wanted to do it, I think she wanted to take back some control over what was happening to her. In fact she almost seemed sadistically happy that she has taken back the power.

As she sat down on the chair, I draped a towel around her shoulders and checked one final time that she was sure she wanted to do this. Mum had now psyched herself up, so she just told me to get on with it. I on the other hand, was an absolute wreck.

Was I ready to do this? Absolutely not.

Was I going to do it? I guess when I heard the buzzing and saw the blade run through the back of mum's hair, my decision was already made.

It took around all of five minutes to cut mums hair. Once I had turned off the clippers, I stood back and was once again choked by emotion. My silence screamed louder than any words could. We had now welcomed our newsiest reality, my mum was bald.

There wasn't a strand of hair left on her head. The absence of her hair made her look even more tiny and frail. Admittedly she looked incredibly cute, she looked like a tiny new born bird. I smile at the thought now, but in that moment I couldn't because it became real. Mum wasn't just unwell in my head, she now looked unwell too. It was a very hard image to compose and one I hadn't prepared for.

That was finally it, mum had swung back at the disease and she'd landed her first punch in her fight. She'd regained her balance and was back in control. Mum had chosen to cut what was going to be torn away from her. She'd made that choice; she chose to change her appearance. Cancer had no say this time around.

"We'll get you a bandana with a fringe attached," was dad's first comment and it literally depicts our family and foreshadowed most of the reactions she received. As a family, we honestly do have an inability to be serious.

As soon as the initial shock of the hair loss wore off, it was surprising how quickly mum's new image became normal. We all loved rubbing her head, she most definitely didn't love it but it made her laugh every time so it was worth it, just to see that.

My sister had two nicknames for mum, now that she was rocking her new image. There are various amazing hairless women who would have been a complete privilege to be compared to but, remember my family have the inability to be serious?

Mum was compared to none other than Gollum and Yoda. Strangely, as soon as the comparisons were made, the resemblance was uncanny.

Mum loved it though, she laughed when Kelly first said it: I mean we all did because it was funny. At no point were we going to allow mum to feel sad about this. She may have looked different to what we were used to, but she was still the same person, the same woman. She was still the same mother.

I honestly believe if we had of treated her as if she was ill and sick, she would have deteriorated. I am fully aware that she was ill and sick, she was fighting cancer but it didn't mean she should be treated any different.

Mum was diagnosed with cancer, she was fighting with cancer. Under no circumstances was she cancer. That's the issue with labels; people easily become defined by them. Mum was not going to be defined by cancer. Mum was so much more and deserves to be seen as more than somebody who was ill.

You hear it a lot when people try and explain or describe somebody with mental health issues for example. He or she is Bipolar, they're schizophrenic or they're depressed. These small phrases, that most of us are guilty of using, (including me before my own struggles) can be more damaging to someone's wellbeing than I think we realise.

A person who has bipolar, schizophrenia, depression or any other illness shouldn't be identified by their illness. They have the illness yes, and it is a part of them but under no circumstances does it define who they are. If we treat people this way and stigmatise them, how can we expect them to live with their conditions? This is why we never treated mum differently, she had cancer but she was still mum, she just had a little more to love.

We now had nicknames for her and suggestions of how to keep her tiny head warm. I think it's safe to say, we were beginning to accept the newest reality check served to us. Although, not everyone was as accepting to mums new appearance. The grandchildren took a little longer to normalise to it.

They were told and knew about mum's cancer, but they probably didn't understand the full extent of the battle their nan was facing. In some respects, this was actually for the best. They didn't need the worry, stress and upset we all had, especially at their age. In this instance I think innocence was bliss.

We were aware of how difficult it was for people. We noticed that visits were not as regular as they once were. I understand it completely: I get it. I lived with mum so I know just how upsetting and devastating it was to see her like this and to be honest so did she. In fairness, I think those that chose not come in made the right decision, because being upset around her would have been worse. My sister's eldest son, Harry in particular, hated the image of his nan this way. Since birth, he lived with us on and off because he was such a nanny's boy; she wrapped him up in cotton wool.

He couldn't do any wrong, she wouldn't have it. He was the apple of her eye and her little angel. I used to love winding him up; we have more of a sister and brother relationship opposed to aunt and nephew, so I would aggravate him rotten. Despite at the time it being hilarious, when mum stepped in, guess which one of us came off worse?

However, like I said there were many people who hated the sight of mum being so poorly. The fact she had no hair, made the image more dramatic. After a while though, it was so normal that people adapted to her appearance and her new image became old news.

<u>Chapter Five – First Christmas</u>

Mum had her treatment early in December, and wasn't due the next round until the New Year. We were all thankful for this because mum could now enjoy Christmas, without suffering the side effects of her treatment.

We had dealt with a really terrible ending to our year so far. We needed something to pull us back up and through into the next year. We needed a little piece of happiness in the middle of all of our sadness and tiredness.

We've never really been a family who celebrate Christmas in a big and lavish way. All the grandkids would be visited on Christmas Eve; so on the actual day, there would only be myself, mum and dad. We're not really the type of family to do Christmas with every family member we have.

Mum and dad would normally be awake earlier than me. They both have extremely early body clocks. I on the other hand, would typically wake up between 9 and 10 o'clock. By which time, dinner would be prepped and ready to be cooked. Despite mum and dad being awake for a lot longer than me, all the presents would all still be wrapped and organised into our own piles. After we finished opening our gifts together and played around with them; dad would run around, picking up all the ripped and scattered paper.

Whilst dinner was cooking, I would get ready for the day. Of course just how it should be celebrated, I would bathe and put on a fresh pair of pyjamas. Nothing is more festive than a new pair of Christmas pyjamas.

Dinner was typically ready to devour at around 12 o'clock. Dad would always start cooking the meat way before mum woke up, meaning our dinners were always early. I know most people pull out all the stops for their Christmas dinners, but all we do is, add a few pigs in blankets to our normal Sunday roast, (like I said, never been a family to celebrate Christmas big.)

After dinner, all of us were normally food drunk and physically unable to move. I'd sprawl on one sofa, mum would take the other and dad usually took his position on the floor. Whilst we try and breathe through our bloated states, we'd watch a Christmas film. Our favourite is Oliver Twist, then like dominos, we all begin to nod off and surrender to the food coma.

Why do we all do this on Christmas? We all completely over indulge. As soon as December hits, every single excuse is; 'oh its Christmas why not?' It doesn't even matter what the situation is. The excuse is always, 'it's Christmas after all.'

Christmas day is of course the worst day for it, regardless of how full we are, nothing will keep us away from eating disgusting amounts of chocolate and sweets. We make ourselves feel completely sick but hey, it's Christmas after all.

All in all, a stereotypical Christmas day for us would be simple and chilled. Endless amounts of food and drink and really awful TV. It was bliss. I know that to some, this will sound horrifically boring. Most families probably have majority of the extended family over, play games, drinks galore and the full shebang.

I have always loved the idea of that and I've always wanted the typical American Christmas. With snow everywhere you look, have every family member over for dinner, more presents than an elf's workshop and so many decorations, that you can't see your house.

The Christmas after mum's diagnosis was the closest I have got to that. It was completely different to our usual celebration. This year it wasn't just the three of us. We had my aunt Tracey, uncle Darren and cousins Becky and Courtney join us.

We still spent the morning at our own houses unwrapping presents, but by 12 o'clock we were all together. Although having so many people in our living room on Christmas day, was strikingly different, it felt surprisingly normal.

Our two families have always been close and still are to this present day. Tracey is mum's youngest sister and after losing my nan; mum became the mother figure in Tracey's life. Becky and Courtney even refer to her as their nan, instead of their aunt. To others this was confusing, but to us it was nothing but normal.

It's fair to say mum was certainly the head of the family. The person who you would go to for advice, for a gossip but she was also the person you avoid if you're in trouble. Mum played a mother figure to most and I guess, that's why everyone took the news of her having cancer quite hard.

Tracey in particular didn't want to accept the fact mum was unwell. To her, mum was completely normal (just with a bald head.) Obviously, she knew she was poorly but she refused to treat her any different. She would still insist mum made the tea, do her own house work and everything else that others claimed she wasn't well enough to do.

Back to Christmas day, it was a real family occasion; in comparison to how it normally was for us (in the least bar humbug sense possible.) I was so excited to play games, something that always made me slightly envious of when I would see it in other families. I obviously loved my Christmas's with mum and dad, but trying to play a game with only three people loses enjoyment surprisingly quickly.

As mum's appetite had shrunken due to treatment, her food portions looked more like the left over's. We never forced her to eat more than she could stomach. Her taste buds were affected too. She complained on many occasions how things tasted different, or had no taste what so ever. Christmas dinner was no different; her portion was big enough to fit on a child's plate and she still struggled to finish it.

Christmas dinner was done but unlike our usual ritual, we couldn't fall into our food comas and sleep (it would have been rude to sleep when we had company.) Instead we decided to play some games (yay!)

We played a game of word association and Tracey explained the rules to everyone. All you had to do was name a fruit, beginning with the letter of the alphabet on your turn (now really, the rules and premise of the game was quite simple.) Tracey started us off with: apple, followed by banana, and then it was mum's turn. Two letters in and two fruits down, as mum was third working out which letter was next, was incredibly simple right? No wrong!

We all expected the next fruit to be: cherry, coconut or maybe cranberries. I don't think my mother understood the game to be honest. Her answer for a fruit, beginning with the letter C was... orange.

We were all in hysterics, how can somebody get something so wrong? Something as simple as naming a fruit, beginning with the letter C, I should have predicted her answer. When mum was asked questions like this, instead of thinking for a second, she would just say the first thing that popped into her head. Playing riddles with her was hysterical every time.

My friend had a fancy dress party one year and the theme was: 'something beginning with, the first letter, of your first name.' Obviously this meant, I would need to dress as something, beginning with the letter *J*. There were a number of things I could have dressed as. A jockey, Jasmin the Disney princess, a jester and so on (I eventually wore a diy Jesus costume.) However, before I had my costume idea, I asked mum for some inspiration.

I explained the theme to mum and without a second thought, she blurted out: "go as a tree." That's correct, despite me explaining the concept, and her knowing my name, the answer she had was a tree (it's not even remotely close.)

Those moments of her inability to think before she speaks, still make me howl with laughter. She had no idea just how funny she was, it was natural, which always made it ten times funnier.

We quickly changed what game we played. Mum would have needed at least, forty rounds of word association before she knew what to do. This time me and my cousin Becky played a good old game of: 'Who am I?' That wasn't before mum stole the show again. After she royally messed the word association game up, mum began desert preparation: mince pies and cream (cue one of my favourite memories from this day.)

As mum got up from the sofa to prepare desert, she wobbled a little on her feet. She tried her best to stagger out of the wobble; it was like she was, walking over wet marbles (it seemed to last forever.) Then before we knew it, she was sprawled out on the floor, she had gone completely arse over tit.

After we all checked that she was ok, none of us could contain the laughter anymore. We were all in hysterics at this point and mum was still on the floor, which only made it worse. As there was hardly anything of her, she fell down like a feather. Thankfully she didn't hurt anything but her pride. Eventually she got back up and started to prepare the deserts. We however, were all still in fits of laughter.

Mum came back in with her and Tracey's mince pies and cream. She sat back down on the sofa, with Tracey sat in front of her, on the floor. As payback for laughing so much at her, mum threw cream from her desert into Tracey's hair.

Despite being the oldest in the room, mum was undeniably the most immature. None of us tried to stop it; instead we all encouraged it and tried to start a food fight between them. Mum was enjoying every second of it. For the first time in a long time she was genuinely happy.

Tracey on the other hand, wasn't too happy about having cream in her hair. She disappeared into the kitchen and came back in with a yogurt. Within seconds the lid was off and it was all over mum's head. Mum's poor bald head was covered in yogurt, one that had just come out of the fridge.

Mum shouted from the shock and called Tracey some interestingly colourful pet names. At this point, all of us were set off again, doubled over in laughter. We were in that state of deep laughter, where no sound actually comes out. Your mouth is just open and you shake uncontrollably, and take the occasional intake of air (you know the laugh!)

To be honest we spent most of the day like this. It was perfect and without a shadow of doubt, it was the best Christmas day I have had. Seeing how poorly, weak and fragile mum had been in the past months hurt. The sadness I had in my heart was heavy. Then to watch mum laugh, smile, be silly and just be happy, was the best present I had received. All day her smile was wide and her eyes were full with warmth.

Although she was really unwell, my heart swelled knowing that cancer wasn't winning that day. For that day it didn't exist and she was just her: free.

Chapter Six: In Remission

If mum's treatment worked, she would be in remission from this monstrous disease. It didn't mean she was completely cured though. After mum's last chemotherapy session; tests needed to be done, in order to determine whether or not her remission was either partial or complete.

Mum's last session was in the January of 2013. Her sessions had been spread across a six month period; with each one scheduled every three weeks. The breaks in between gave her body a chance to rest and deal with any side effects.

Considering the destruction cancer causes, the treatment itself is not as invasive as you may think. Chemotherapy is simply an IV line flushing a drug through the blood. It's not the treatment that is the problem, it's the side effects. They are aggressive and brutal.

They attack the body and change the person's appearance at a devastating speed (but it's not only the body and appearance that take a battering.) We all recognise the most common side effect being hair loss (which, on its own merit, is completely life altering and devastating.) However, it's not the worst by a long stretch, their personality becomes under attack too.

Mum had quite a number of side effects from the treatment. The first major one of course was: the hair loss and it happened sooner than I expected. The hair loss for mum wasn't actually a massive ordeal. To her it was simply a black and white issue, unlike us who were devastated. Obviously she would have preferred to keep her hair, but to her it was only hair and it would grow back, you see it wasn't the first time mum had lost her hair.

She had alopecia as a teenager, so the emotional attachment to her hair had been softened by that experience. Her hair grew back then, so she saw this as not being any different.

Aside from the hair loss, her appetite declined with little desire to eat; leading to noticeable weight loss. Before mum had any health issues, she had always been a well filled out woman. As a previously curvy size 16 lady with a chubby face, she gradually dropped the weight when her health issues began. Her dress size fell down slowly, before her size became a stagnant 10-12. She still had some of her curves but they were definitely less plump and most noticeably was the shape of her face. It was once rounded but it became drawn in with the weight loss.

During her chemotherapy treatment, her weight continued to plummet. It was weight that she couldn't really afford to lose, but she quickly fell down to a tiny size 6-8. It didn't look healthy, she was practically skin and bones, her face had shrunken even more. Every bone became highlighted under her skin; it looked like her face had collapsed inside itself.

Her mouth was constantly sore and laced with ulcers, which made eating even harder for her. Her taste buds had become redundant and she often complained how everything tasted like metal or cardboard. The only things that she never lost her appetite for was sweet things. Give her a cream cake over a roast dinner and she would have asked for seconds (her addiction to tea also never ceased either.)

Mum was also in constant pain and irritation with her skin too. As the chemotherapy had left it visibly dry and scaly, we had to moisturise her body from head to toe often. The worst part was as the skin was so sore; the constant application of moisturiser made it a painful experience.

On top of everything, mum's energy had been drained. It was especially noticeable each time she had the treatment. As soon as she came home from the hospital, she would go straight to sleep for hours. A good thing about her sleeping as soon as she came home was she never really suffered with nausea. There were the odd days where she felt sick, but never to the extreme others do and she never physically vomited.

The side effects were brutal and they would weaken the strongest of people. They certainly weakened my mother. She was so frail; the slightest touch would hurt her, making it hard to help her. Her mobility was probably affected the worst; she needed assistance getting in and out of the bath, out of bed and down the stairs. Walking would drain her entirely and her steps were slower than a child learning how to walk. She was dependant on help and it absolutely frustrated her.

Being an independent woman she prided herself on relying only on herself. Therefore having to be helped in and out of the bath, and at times carried to bed, embarrassed her. She hated it and we hated knowing how distressed she was. A typically stubborn woman, asking for help from anyone was a trait she was foreign to (regardless how much she needed it.)

It wasn't just the physical changes we had to watch mum suffer with. All of the changes to her body had an impact on her as a person too. Normally a very happy and quick witted woman, she became snappy and irritable. I would even go as far as saying she became miserable, and at times unbearable to be around. Her quick wit turned into an acid tongue, making your blood run cold in seconds.

Her words sometimes were laced with such venom you would physically flinch on their impact. None of this was her fault of course. She wasn't and never was a spiteful person before this ordeal, but this was just how she dealt with her frustrations and annoyance towards her inability to do things herself. Although, it did make living with her at times a true nightmare, but I never took anything she did or said to heart. I knew it wasn't her, this disease was stripping her of the qualities we all adored and it replaced them with what felt like evil. My mother was fighting a battle with cancer, but she was also battling a tougher fight, with herself.

Everything she was slowly became more distant, and what she used to be able to do, she no longer could. Of course this would affect anyone of us. Dad took the brunt of most of her frustration; he practically became her full time carer. He carried her to bed, lifted her in and out of the bath, cooked, and cleaned, all whilst working full time. He never once second guessed it or complained. She was the woman he loved and to him this was a responsibility he had to her.

Having to watch the woman who when you was growing up; worked two to three jobs, from: fruit picking, factory work to cleaning, become so weak that it took her two to three minutes to walk to the bathroom was heart wrenching. I hated seeing her struggle so much; this wasn't the woman I was used to. I only knew the woman who would walk anywhere and do anything. I didn't know the woman who was a frail structure of skin and bones, wanting to stay at home because she was too embarrassed and weak to go anywhere, and that ripped my heart to shreds.

I was at university all throughout mum's treatment, which mum and dad were both incredibly proud of. It was something I was very proud of and excited about as well. Yet it was also a time where I became familiar with the feeling of anxiety. It was in my second year when mum became ill, so I decided to do the commute to London and stay at home. It was draining, but I couldn't have been anywhere else whilst she was going through everything at home.

Thankfully mum's treatment had worked and her tests had come back confirming her remission was complete and not partial. It obviously didn't mean she was out of the woods; she still needed regular check-ups to ensure she remained in remission. For us though this was it, she had got rid of the cancer and we finally had her back.

Despite the cancer being treated, mum's health didn't improve, she didn't regain weight and she was still a small, frail size 6-8. Her food portions never increased, her mobility was still impaired and she was still very weak. The woman I grew up with, the curvaceous, quick witted and fiercely independent woman I knew my whole life had gone and I faced a new reality.

She was still the same person, she was still my mother but she was just now packaged slightly different. It wasn't a factor of her not wanting to be that fierce woman anymore; it was simply a factor of not being physically able to.

As her frame remained delicate and frail, she also remained constantly cold. There wasn't a single time she wasn't cold. Her hands and feet were like slabs of ice, her body constantly shivering, trying to naturally warm up. Even on warm days she would be dressed for winter. She never left the house without having numerous layers of clothes on, a scarf and coat. Her hands would literally turn mauve, and because dad and I are always warm, we would have to use our hands to warm hers up.

We would take her icy hands in ours, circling them in our palms to try and warm them up, but due to her arthritis we had to be gentle. Slowly you would see the colour come back to her skin but, they still remained cold at all times. It got to the stage where no matter where she was, whether it was at home or out in public, she would need a hot water bottle. This was one of the only ways she could stay warm. If she was cold and couldn't warm up she needed to go somewhere that was warm and have a tea and refill her water bottle.

My graduation ceremony was a perfect example. I studied at Greenwich University, so we had to travel up to the campus. The campus is located directly next to the River Thames and my graduation was held in May 2013 in the late afternoon. It was absolutely freezing this day (even I will admit to that.) Of course mum and dad both came, they were over the moon that I had graduated.

Our ceremony was streamed live to a room for all the families and people who came to support, so mum and dad were able to see the full service. I had a quick photo with my dad before I headed into the hall. Mum refused to have a picture taken because she hated the way she looked. When I finally came out, we had a class of 2013 photograph. Then we all proceeded to find our friends to get a photo in our gowns. Everyone's parents and guests were all bursting with pride. Everywhere you looked there were pictures being taken, family pictures that would probably be pride and centre of their homes. I was looking around this huge campus grounds for mum and dad. I knew that mum would have been absolutely freezing cold and was most probably inside somewhere.

I called dad to see where they were, and it turns out they had to go to a pub about ten minutes from campus to get mum warmed up. They missed my whole graduation ceremony and I had nobody other than my university friends to take pictures with. My heart sank if I'm totally honest.

I obviously do not hold it against them, mum wasn't in a well state of health and that meant more to me than anything. I just wished for that one day, she was well enough to watch me graduate and be there to take a picture with, just like everyone else.

After mum's battle with cancer, her health conditions seemed to multiply. Doctors and hospital appointments were almost a weekly ritual for her and she was on unsettling amounts of medication. She had on-going issues with her thyroid, she had brittle bones as well as rheumatoid arthritis and she was also diagnosed with COPD. These are just a handful of the health issues I can remember from the top of my head (if I wrote them all, I would need the whole book.)

Mum's health deterioration continued for years, she became less and less of the woman I grew up with. Regardless of how frail she was, she was still the woman you feared getting into trouble with though. She was still the woman who could bring every possible fear you have to the surface with that one look. Fundamentally, she was exactly who she always was, but at the same time she was different.

Her mobility had severely deteriorated; she became so fragile and weak that she had to eventually rely on a wheelchair. This was something that really affected her, she absolutely despised it. The reality of having to use a wheelchair embarrassed her so much, she resented going out and would always try to avoid going out in public. Mum hated the thought of her looking as unwell as she actually was and knowing people could see.

As a woman who once fell down our stairs, from top to bottom and broke her leg (only to hobble back up to bed and go to sleep,) become a woman who couldn't walk from the living room to the bathroom, without becoming breathless, was a tough reality to face.

To go from a woman who was once able to peel, cut and cook the best roast potatoes I have ever tasted, to a woman who couldn't open a can of beans because of her arthritis, was a devastating new normality to accept.

Watching the woman you grew up thinking was indestructible, almost superhuman, become a fragile shell, completely dependent on everyone and constantly unwell, was absolutely heart breaking. It was actually gut wrenching to be perfectly honest.

Chapter Seven– Nil By Mouth

Due to all of mum's health issues, when she got poorly she really had a bad time with it. It really took the wind out from under her, and a simple cold could wipe her out for weeks. However, being the stubborn and strong-headed woman she was, when she got ill she would refuse to go to a doctor or hospital (why do particular generations not use the services available when needed? It amazes me.)

Despite having so many health problems; that she could have kept a doctor in their job just by treating her alone. "I'll be alright," "It's only," and "It'll go soon" were the normal responses you heard from mum when we would ask her to see the doctor.

One of the health issues mum had was acid reflux: she would have to limit what she ate in case it irritated the reflux. When it flared up she would be in immense discomfort and pain. Her stomach would bloat and would have to drink endless amounts of boiled water, just to relieve some of the trapped air. On the bad days she would be nauseated with it too, along with not being able to pass stools properly (I understand I'm not making this sound very glamorous, but hey, warts and all!)

What's the reason for this brief medical history lesson?

Well, in the week of the 28th December 2015, mum had her usual symptoms of her reflux. Her stomach was so bloated; it looked like she was eight months pregnant. It was visible to how uncomfortable she was. It had an impact on her mobility too, she struggled on the best of days but she really struggled this week.

Obviously when we suggested going to the doctors, it fell upon deaf ears. Instead she decided to suffer in pain and discomfort, which continued into the weekend. Mum had bought a bottle of laxatives from the chemist, because she was struggling to go to the toilet. Now, I'm no doctor but even I know that this is a risky treatment to try out, especially with the challenge with mobility.

As me and dad had work commitments, we couldn't give mum the full time care she needed, when and if she was poorly. However, my sister would pop in until dad finished work, so someone was home with her at all times. If my sister wasn't already here in the mornings, I would wake up and get mum out of bed and help her down the stairs. I'd take her to the toilet and back to the sofa, make her a cup of tea and some breakfast. Then I would finally prepare the endless amounts of medication for her (I swear at times she would rattle like a pill bottle.)

Monday the 4th January 2016, was a typical day of that routine:

-I helped mum out of bed and downstairs.

-Took her to the toilet.

-Made her a cup of tea.

-Made toast for breakfast.

-Got together all the medication.

All ticked off.

When it hit 9:30 I needed to go to work. Mum was lying on the sofa, watching breakfast television. I didn't want to leave her to be honest, but she assured me she was ok. I had a small sense of security from the knowledge that dad was due home at 1:30pm. At best it was around three hours until dad came home. Plus like I said, she kept insisting she was ok.

Time skip to 6:30pm, I had finished work and as I walked through the door, mum was still lying on the sofa. Mum was so poorly this day that she hadn't moved until dad had come home. She couldn't even go to the toilet as she was unable to move. My heart completely sunk to my stomach. I had left her at 9:30am that morning and went to work as if everything was normal. Except for mum it wasn't, she felt so poorly but never mentioned it. (Her stubbornness was so irritating.)

This will always lie heavy on my shoulders and heart. That morning I should have realised she wasn't well and stayed home to make sure she was ok. However I didn't, I went to work. Mum was left alone until dad got back, she hadn't had anything to eat or drink since breakfast and she couldn't even make it to the toilet. She was completely shaken up.

This woman was so proud, to rely on anyone to do something for her like: walk her to the toilet, was soul destroying. This day really took something away from her, I think she accepted that she was poorly and needed the help and assistance now. She had to accept she could no longer be independent, much to her disliking.

If I'm honest mum was embarrassed, she was vulnerable and bare, concepts usually alien to her. Mum's cousin Bev (who I called aunt,) had popped in to visit and mum still wasn't ok. We all had a shock when mum looked at dad and said: "I think I should go to the hospital." For her to suggest and voluntarily want to go to hospital, meant something was seriously not right. She was scared and it showed.

When we arrived at the hospital, mum got in her wheelchair so she didn't have to try to walk. At this point, mum started to look increasingly poorly, uncomfortable and completely exhausted.

I couldn't give specific times of when we arrived, to when we was seen etc. What I do know is like any hospital visit; it was hours of waiting room boredom. We had to sit in the A&E waiting room surrounded by at least twenty other people. Some looked worse for wear and some looked like they just needed a bed to sleep their hangover off.

One thing I will say, an A&E waiting room can be a great place for entertainment and despite being so unwell, it was mum who supplied most of the entertainment.

When I stated before that my whole family love winding people up and tormenting people, what I failed to mention is my mother was the worst for it (especially to strangers.) Her favourite victims were men, I think she enjoyed watching them crumble and being embarrassed.

So let's discuss the waiting room antics... please do remember that in the following anecdotes: myself, my aunt and my father were all present throughout (along with a whole room of strangers.) I'll start by painting the picture of us in the room.

Surprisingly we all managed to sit together; mum was neatly parked up on the end of the row in her wheelchair. She was completely living the dream to be fair: a blanket, hot water bottle and a tea; whereas the rest of us fidgeted left to right, every minute trying to get comfortable. Trying to evenly spread the time sat on each bum cheek, to avoid one side going numb.

Directly opposite us, in the corner of a doorway and facing into the waiting room, was a gentleman in his mid to late thirties. He was in a hospital wheelchair and had a head dressing which was stained with blood at the front.

The poor bloke clearly had been in the wars. Aside from his head injury, he was covered in cuts and scratches too. He was wearing a blue sports jacket, which was half on and half on. It became quite evident that he was intoxicated. He was frustrated of waiting; getting up every five minutes like a Jack in the box.

At one point he played Eminem on his phone, it was so loud we all heard each breath Eminem took between his lyrics. Although it grounded him for a while and occupied his frustration, it didn't last that long. He attempted to stand but his wheelchair moved and smashed into the wall. Now I've always been a person who lets people live, if it's not affecting me directly, let people be. Mum however, definitely wasn't the same. If something or somebody pissed her off, she would make it known. A quality I'm half envious of but half thankful of not having.

Anyway, after fidgeting Pete had now practically smashed up the wall in the waiting room. A familiar voice cuts through the waiting room mumbles, demanding for the guy to: "sit fucking still." That familiar voice belonged to none other than my mother. Imagine a complete stranger saying this to you, I honestly do not know how she got away with it so much.

We were all completely embarrassed and told her through gritted teeth to shut up and leave him alone. A typical panicked and British reaction to when you feel uncomfortable. A number of the other patients around us had smirks across their faces though. They were all trying to hold their laughs in. It still makes me smile to this day; she literally said what everyone else was thinking.

What made the situation even funnier was, this poor bloke simply repositioned his wheelchair and sat back down. He didn't say a word, he simply listened to what mum said and obeyed. I was completely and utterly gobsmacked. This stranger had actually done what she asked him to do; I was fully expecting him to politely tell her to get lost but he didn't.

I mean, for me I wouldn't dream of second guessing or doing as I was told but, that's because I knew the consequences and they weren't worth it. Yet this stranger never knew her, maybe he just sensed it. It's definitely the look, the one only mother's know how to do.

A good amount of time had passed and of course in a waiting room, there's only so much small talk you can do and only a few trips to the shop, before you run out of ways to pass the time. When mum was finally called, dad wheeled her into the triage room. Within the time mum went in to be seen, more patients were filling up the empty seats.

Two of the new patients were prisoners each escorted by two guards. As soon as I saw the prison officers, I had instant dread. No not because I'm an escaped inmate, but because of the fascination my mother had for men in uniform. *Great*, this is all this waiting room needed, my sixty three year old mother, dirty talking to a prison officer.

Mum eventually came back out and was wheeled back to her spot. The doctor had concerns about her ankles. There was a lot of water retention and he felt it could be a problem with her heart. They wanted to run some tests, to find out what was going on and to rule out any complications with her heart. That was the update, so we knew we were in for a long wait.

I notice when dad was wheeling mum's chair back, she had spotted the prison officers standing adjacent to us. I couldn't help but smile to myself because I knew what was about to proceed (cue internal dread.)

I would like to at this stage, point out two things, firstly: the waiting room now had roughly twenty to twenty five people in. Secondly my mother, who could barely put a sentence together when we came to hospital, was now blushing at the sight of a man in uniform. Almost like a kid in a candy shop.

"Hello handsome," mum shouted across the waiting room in the direction of the prison officer. We tried warning her to leave the poor guy alone, but it fell on deaf ears. She sat there grinning from ear to ear. She knew what she was doing; her ability to embarrass grown men was a work of art.

This poor prison officer was a baby compared to my, sixty three year old, praying mantis of a mother. He was no older than mid-twenties and stood around 5.7" possibly taller. His head was covered in shaven stubble and I guess he had a charming face (I personally didn't see the appeal.) The poor sod looked up and just politely smiled at mum. He was clearly nervous and uneasy about the situation. I watched him bend down and pick up a magazine scanning over the pages, desperately wanted to hide.

I've seen this trick before, I've done it in fact. When you're in an awkward setting, invited somewhere by your friend and they're the only one who you know. They then decide to walk away to catch up with someone they know. The first thing you do to comfort your awkwardness, is get your phone out and find something else to distract your attention. Hoping it disguises your presence, hoping nobody tries talking to you. That's what the poor prison officer tried to do. He wanted to hide behind this magazine and to become invisible.

"Oi handsome, I'm talking to you. You're bloody lovely you are."

That was her next attempt at getting his attention, no shame what so ever. At this point, the whole waiting room was filled with strangers smirking, with some actually laughing at her. She loved every single second of it, she was like an entertainer and the whole room, was in the palms of her hands.

The poor guy was now being laughed at by his accompanying colleague, and the prisoner being transported. Probably not the greatest of things for him, he'd be the laughing stock of the prison when he returned. I can imagine it: everyone tormenting him at work because he was hit on by a 60 year old floozy.

Once again, he was polite in his response, but a lot more awkward than before. He quickly muttered: "hi, you ok?" before trying to escape back into the magazine.

"Come here babe, come sit with me." Her final comment before she broke this poor man's blood pressure. With that comment, the whole waiting room broke out in laughter; including the poor prison officer. Noticeably shy and embarrassed, he handed the magazine to the other officer and walked out the exit. "Christine, you've made the poor man blush. Leave off you wind up." Dad advised mum through a widened smile.

"What I'm only playing? He must be gay." Her response caused an eruption of even more laughter. I couldn't help but laugh alongside them, she was on a roll. Although, part of me felt a slight sense of empathy for the poor man, but she was funny and it was all in jest. To be fair, this was the first time in hours I saw her smile and laugh, so to me his embarrassment was totally worth it. Thankfully for him, she did leave him alone after that. She had her fun and torment, he was now safe.

After hours of waiting, mum was eventually seen again by another doctor. We were told that they were going to admit her for the night. They still needed to run some tests to see what was going on.

The porter escorted us to the ward mum was staying in for the night. We got her comfortable in her bed and waited with her while observations were taken. I don't particularly remember times if I'm honest, I just know it was late. I had work in the morning, so I said goodnight to mum and told her that I would be back tomorrow. Dad stayed with her, partly because he didn't want to leave her but, equally because she didn't want to be left on her own.

As I left, mum asked me to put together a bag of clothes and toiletries, so she could freshen up the next day. This was the first thing I did when I got home. I was so tired that if I didn't do it then I would have forgotten. I didn't sleep well that night either, I couldn't settle knowing she was staying in hospital overnight. A place she hated so much.

I had dosed off at some point, as I remember being woken up by my alarm clock at 7:30 in the morning. It felt like I had only been asleep for ten minutes. I called dad to find out how she was and if there was any update to when she would be coming home.

Dad said she needed to stay in until Wednesday because they were still running tests. After speaking with dad, I called my manager and explained what had happened and he agreed for me to have the day off. So I called dad straight back and told him I was coming straight to the hospital.

As I got to the ward, I was told that mum was now nil-by-mouth and would be having an operation on Wednesday. They needed to drain fluid from her stomach as this was the reason she was so poorly. This had escalated quicker than I expected, it had turned from being bloated to needing an operation.

Chapter Eight– Nil By Mouth Part II

Nil-by-mouth: a medical instruction meaning to withhold food and fluids. A Latin phrase which translates literally to English as: nothing through the mouth (thank you Google.)

Before the doctor said mum was nil-by-mouth, dad had brought her a fresh cream cake from the shop. Much to my surprise it was still wrapped, on the table by her bed when I got there in the morning. Dad needed the toilet and when he left to find one, mum asked me to pass her the cake. I reminded her she wasn't allowed anything to eat yet.

"I'm not going to eat it, I just want to look at it," was the response I got (this woman really thought I was an idiot.) Obviously I knew it was a complete and utter lie. However, I looked at the wrapper and said to myself: *unless someone undoes this for her, she isn't getting into that.*

Due to her arteritis she couldn't open a packet of crisps, so there wasn't a chance of her getting past the cake wrapper. I passed her the cake and started unpacking her things I had brought with me. I glanced over at her when I heard the rustling of the packet and chuckled at her desperate attempts of getting into the cake. I continued unpacking her things and thankfully the rustling did eventually stop (clearly admitting defeat…or so I thought.)

"Erm Christine, what you doing? You're nil-by-mouth." As soon as I heard my dad say this sentence, I spun my head around to look at her. She had cream all around her mouth while her jaw snapped up and down. "Mother, you're not supposed to be eating. How the hell did you even get that open?" In complete shock (and admiration of her determination,) I just laughed at her and wiped the cream off her mouth.

"I'm starving. They can't expect me not to eat for that long. It'll be fine, just don't tell them" was her response. I don't know how she expected us not to tell medical experts, that my rebellious mother (who is supposed to be nil-by-mouth,) had just devoured a cream cake.

"Miss Wilkins, we need to take your obs. Are you ready for us?"

Great, well if we don't tell them, then sky high blood sugars will.

"Erm, mum forgot she was nil-by-mouth and, I just got here, but she just ate that." I nervously pointed to the cake expecting to be told off.

The nurse started to giggle and walked closer to mum, took her hand and gave it a light tap. "Forgot did we, Miss Wilkins? Why do I find that hard to believe? What are we going to do with you hmm? You're going to be trouble aren't you? I'll have to let the doctors know, but your operation will probably need to be postponed."

As the nurse went to leave she let another giggle out. Mum had already managed to wrap her around her little finger, and she'd only been there for twenty four hours.

Dad however wasn't too impressed, neither was I to be fair but, we couldn't help but smile at her. This woman who like I said, struggles to open a packet of crisps, had literally just smashed through the wrapper of a cream cake. We were only frustrated because she would now have to be in hospital for even longer.

The nurse returned still wearing a massive grin across her face, (it felt like she was about to reprimand her favourite, misbehaving child.) "Right, Miss Wilkins, I've spoken to the doctor and we're going to have to move the operation to Thursday. This means tomorrow, you'll be nil-by-mouth, so, no cream cakes." Mum looked at her with a glee in her eyes, thanked her and clarified "am I still nil-by-mouth today."

"No darling, not nil-by-mouth today," the nurse happily confirmed with a smirk.

"Oh I'll have a cup of tea then when you're ready babe, I'm gasping." I couldn't help but laugh at her cheekiness. How she got away with being such a git I have no idea. Yet despite it, she still managed to get people falling in love with her and, they would bend over backwards trying to accommodate whatever she needed. Low and behold, mum soon had a cup of tea by her side and the rest of the cream cake (she was living her best life as the kids say today.)

With mum being kept in, the news spread fast and dad's mobile was ringing left, right and centre with calls and texts seeing how mum was doing. Before we knew it mum's brothers: Paul, Kevin, Steve and Malcolm surrounded her bedside. Now... nobody is more tormenting than mum's brothers, they never take anything seriously and will do anything to hear laughter.

"Come on Chris, move up don't be lazy." The first thing my uncle Kevin said, before sitting on the end of her bed. As he sat down, his eyes scanned the room to find something or someone to aggravate. Soon enough he had found something, the control hooked onto the bottom of mum's bed (I knew what was coming next.)

Mum's legs began to rise in unison along with her upper body, her face was a picture. Pure panic and confusion as her eyes darted around for someone to save her. An enormous cackle invaded the ward and my uncle Kevin was bent over in hysterics. When we all joined in, we sounded like a pack of hyenas, all except mother of course. She was still trapped in the dip of the folded bed, and couldn't do anything, but it didn't take her long to see the funny side.

With a soft giggle mum pleaded (not without profanities thrown in) with Kevin to put the bed back to normal because she couldn't move. This made us laugh even more, but very quickly Kevin did as he was told and mum was slowly repositioned back to normal.

It was refreshing to see my uncles, because it was emotionally tormenting and mentally aggravating being at the hospital. Their presence completely lifted our spirits and in that moment I forgot where I was, it was a much needed release.

My family (myself included to some extent,) are not the greatest at showing our emotions. That's why we're never serious because it's easier to create laughter and smiles, than it is to talk about how we're really feeling. After all laughter is the best medicine, even in the darkest times, humour is the perfect way to remind you that life is actually alright.

Although outsiders may not know how to read us, we know each other's limits and how we feel in situations. I know for a fact that my uncles hated, seeing their sister lying in that hospital bed. Despite causing absolute havoc on the ward and making everyone laugh, the sadness and pain glassed their eyes. They couldn't stand still, neither of them removed their coats and they stood the whole time. I knew they felt helpless and uncomfortable because we all did.

After half an hour of visiting and winding up everyone on the ward, including the poor nurses, my uncles decided to leave and let mum rest. Dad hadn't been home yet and he looked completely exhausted, so he decided to get a lift home with Steve. He wanted to have a quick sleep and a bath. As they all left both me and mum let out a subtle sigh. All of us were shattered, our emotions were working overtime. The stress, concern, worry, laughter and the sadness had completely over worked our bodies and minds.

Within minutes mum had her eyes closed, her mouth was slightly open and her face looked so still and calm. Not too long after, her snores were echoing through the ward. I however struggled to sleep, I wanted to but I just couldn't drift off. I just sat in the chair next to mum, closed my eyes and stayed awake in my mind's darkness.

"The nurse said that they're going to move you upstairs, onto another ward soon." I heard my dad's muffled voice, slowly opening my eyes and rubbing them gently. Dad was back and mum was now sitting up in bed.

"When did you get back?"

I must have eventually nodded off because I didn't hear him return. I was clearly very tired because I can't normally sleep with noise around me. Especially the sound of snoring, it drives me crazy (yes I am one of those people.) I get irritated at abnormally loud noises. If someone breathes too heavy, my mind gets restless to the point I could cry. This is when I'm awake and conscious, so when I'm trying to sleep it gets worse.

"About an hour ago babe, you were both asleep. They're moving mum to a ward upstairs soon."

I slept for an hour. How?

After mum had her observations taken, we were taken to the McCulloch ward on level three of the hospital. The ward was for patients who needed: surgical, urology, breast care and ear, nose and throat procedures. We stood in front of the locked double doors, waiting for the nurse to buzz us through. "Miss Wilkins," the porter relayed into the intercom. Shortly after, the doors slowly separated allowing us entry, and mum was pushed through in her bed like Queen Sheba. Dad and I followed on behind her, carrying her belongings.

The smell of the hospital dinners was thrown up my nostrils as we walked around to the cubical that mum would be staying in. It smelt so bad, *why does hospital food smell like that?* I was holding back the urge to gag, only for it to get stronger when walking past the kitchen area. I had to pull the neck of my top up and over my nose, to inhale my perfume because I would have been sick.

The walk to where mum's cubical was surprisingly long. The ward as a whole was structured like a hockey stick. After entering the double doors, you're led straight down eventually coming to a reception desk positioned on a bend. The rest of the ward then curves to the right until it spills out into a straight corridor (it was huge.)

Mums' cubical was at the end of that corridor. It was difficult not to look around at the other patients who were admitted. It's really awkward when you catch their eye contact though. *Everyone does it. It's human nature, right?* We finally get to where mum was going to be staying, the porter manoeuvred mum and her bed into her designated space, and I glanced around the room. The room was quite spacious. It housed six single beds, three on the left and three on the right, leaving a spacious walk way in the middle.

Each individual cubical was identical. It had a bed, a wooden bedside chair: with navy blue leather covering the cushioned seat and back. Next to the bed stood a cabinet for storage and amenities and finally a blue curtain circled the boundary of the cubicle. Mum's bed was wheeled into the middle space, on the right side of the ward. The bed to the right of her was empty (creepily awaiting company.) Five out of the six beds were now occupied with bodies awaiting their treatment and procedures.

For the next few hours, me and dad sat with mum getting her settled in and watching the nurses take their regular observations. Hospitals are literally the most draining and boring places on earth and you find yourself making ridiculous small talk. It's normally an acceptable exchange with strangers, but not with your nearest and dearest. I don't think you ask if someone is ok, or how they feel, more than when sitting next to someone in a hospital bed.

When it got later into the evening, I decided to go home, get a bath and sleep. Dad stayed with mum because their friends were visiting. I leant over and gave mum a kiss and squeezed her into a hug before exchanging our goodnights. I was so tired; I don't remember getting home, having a bath or even climbing into my bed. All I remembered is how I was rudely awoken the next morning by my alarm screaming into my ear. I'm a serial snoozer and I rely far too much on the ability to steal extra minutes of shut eye. When my ears and mind could no longer stand the screeching alarm, I decided to get up.

With mum being nil-by-mouth all day, I decided to go to work. There was nothing much I could do, plus dad was already at the hospital before I woke up. The normal visiting times started at 10:00am; however once again, my mother had managed to wrap her new nurses around her fingers (including the head nurse who ran the ward.) Therefore, they allowed dad to be the one exception. Mum didn't want a stranger washing her or taking her to the toilet, so my poor exhausted but selfless father did it all.

As he was always there early, he was allowed to have breakfast courtesy of the hospital kitchen (no thank you!) Obviously mum was not allowed any due to her nil-by-mouth status. I called dad in the morning to double check that mum was ok. If I'm totally honest it was to settle the on-going argument in my head, whether or not I should go back into work. Everything was fine, so I got ready and went.

Although I was physically at work, mentally and emotionally I was sat with mum at her bedside. I found myself under time's hypnotic power once again, and have no recollection of what I did at work. All I know is work lasted seven and a half hours and as soon as I finished, I ordered a taxi to the hospital.

Being back at her bedside, I was present again physically, mentally and emotionally. After the, "how was work?" and "how are you?" questions had been asked, we simply sat there enjoying family time. Granted we would have much preferred to be all curled up at home in front of the TV but, for now this was just as good. We were together and I felt a harmony within my body. Mum had done well with obeying the nil-by mouth rule this time around, no cream cake tricks meaning her operation was the next day.

Thursday 7th January 2016: operation day. I didn't go to work, instead was with mum before and after the operation. She looked incredibly cute, her tiny little, five foot nothing frame being completely engulfed by the bed. Her weight didn't even make a dent in the mattress.

After the morning visiting hours had finished, I went home to freshen up and also grab a few fresh clothes for mum too. Dad of course stayed, mum didn't mind who came and left, but she refused to let dad leave if he didn't have to. Her operation was scheduled for 2:00pm in the afternoon and was scheduled to last two hours, although I wanted to be there when she came out, visiting hours to see her was 6:00pm.

I couldn't wait for an additional two hours to see her so I actually went earlier and thankfully the nurses allowed me in (she was the favourite remember!) Dad was still there when I arrived. Due to mum having the operation, they didn't seem to mind us being there early. As I walked into the ward and made my way to mum's cubicle, I heard my sister, niece and nephews. I expected to see mum, but she was still in theatre. The operation had now lasted hours over the initial time we were told.

After hours of waiting impatiently, mum was brought through. Despite her just having surgery, she looked so well. There was a glow to her, one that I hadn't seen on her face for a long time. The first thing she asked was if she had missed dinner time. Safe to say, the operation worked up an appetite. Soon enough, she was devouring a yogurt and a nice cup of tea.

That night I left the hospital absolutely tired but happy and relieved. Mum had the operation finally, and she looked healthier than I'd seen her in ages. Her appetite was back, along with her humour, so it wouldn't be long before she was home. Back home where she belongs, with us.

Chapter Nine –D.N.R

Friday 8th January.

I wake up to my screaming 7:30am alarm; I began mourning my sleep I was so deeply enjoying. I've come to the conclusion that, it's called morning because really, what we're doing is actually mourning the sleep we've just been ripped from.

Anyone who knows me will tell you explicitly, I am not a morning person at all. I like to have at least an hour to myself, just so I can be angry at the fact I'm not asleep anymore. I've never truly understood the importance of wanting to converse so early in the morning either. It's just best to leave me alone in the morning.

Dad had already left for the hospital, he was completely exhausted but he would never put his needs before us. Mum wanted him at the hospital all the time and that's exactly what he did.

I spent majority of my morning in the bathroom getting ready for work (plus it's my favourite room in the world.) I left for work at 9:30am, taking my normal route, stopping off at the shop to get a can of Red Bull. I needed caffeine and although it didn't give me wings, it surely gave my eyes the support they needed to stay open.

The walk to work is only a ten minute stroll at best, so I normally get to work earlier than my starting hours, it's a good way to shake my morning mood off too. Typically when I get to work, I spend time catching up with everyone about our evenings. Discussing what we all watched, what we had for dinner (by now I am finally warming to human contact again.)

I am a team leader of a sales team at the Daily Telegraph, it can be really stressful at times but 90% of the time it's enjoyable (mainly because of the people I work with.) I spend every day with my friends, just having endless amounts of fun and laughter. I basically get paid to laugh and smile every day.

Everyone at work was aware that mum was in hospital and this was the first day, I had come to work in good spirits. My mind, body and spirit were all present today. Most people asked how mum was doing, and I smiled each time and told them she was doing well. She had never looked so healthy after her operation.

On a sales floor it's important to make sure morale and atmosphere is as high as possible. Therefore, each morning we would hold briefings, congratulating and acknowledging those who achieved standout performances. It was my turn to present the brief this day and I was in good spirits. I was sarcastic and silly as usual, but I had to be on my best behaviour (no swearing basically,) because our centre manager was there to give an important update afterwards.

I was at least minutes into my briefing when my phone rang. My ringtone is quite distinctive: it's the normal iPhone ringer but breaks into Jay Z and Kanye West – Paris (I know I'm so cool.) Anyway ignoring it, I continued on: if it was important they would ring back or leave a message.

I'm now half way through congratulating the previous day's performers, and my phone had now rung three times. At this point, my heart was beating fast and my mind wasn't concentrating on what I was doing anymore. All I could think about was, who was trying to get hold of me and what could be so urgent. I read out the last stat to my briefing and my phone rang for the fourth time. I looked towards my manager and told him, "I've missed four phone calls and I need to see who it is." He nods and with that I left the briefing area.

The call had ended by the time I got to my phone. I looked at the four missed calls notifications, all from: Papa Bear. Instantly I got a little flutter of butterflies with the excitement at the thought of mum coming home.

I headed to the meeting room situated on the right of the briefing area. Passing my colleagues, who were about to be spoken to by the big boss, I catch the eye of my manager and simply signal that I needed to make a call.

Unlocking my phone, I clicked onto my missed calls and hit in dad's contact. Anticipating his answer, the phone stops ringing and I break into a smile ready to hear his voice. Only all I hear silence. *Maybe his signal is bad? He is at the hospital after all.*

"Hello…what's up? Sorry I missed your calls I was doing the briefing." I explained, only to be met with more deafening silence." Dad…are you alright?" Then the most shattering, painful and gut wrenching words punched through my ears.

"No babe…mum died," followed by his sobbing breath.

I remember pulling the phone down to my cheek and closing my eyes. I needed to process what I was just told.

I couldn't.

This wasn't happening.

Not now.

Not me.

Not us.

Not her.

No, they must have made a mistake.

All I could say back was: "are you joking me?"

I was now starting to panic; my heartbeat was so loud I heard it echo. I didn't just feel it pounding my chest; I felt it in my throat, in my stomach and in my head. I could taste the bile my stomach was retching up into my throat. Then I felt the warm stroke of tears on my face, stopping at my jaw and jumping off onto the floor.

I don't know if dad responded, but the call had ended. Before I knew it, my echoing heartbeat was now silenced by agonizing, crippling and screaming sobs. *Where were these noises coming from?*

I was so confused.

What on earth was happening?

Where the hell am I?

Then it hit me those chilling, heart-breaking screams were mine. I was folded up in a ball on the floor, my back arched on the wall, cradling my legs that were shielding my face. My face completely soaked with hot streaks, leading to my mouth as I screamed silently. My sobs cracked in unison with my heart and my breathing become harder to control.

My whole body felt heavy. I couldn't feel anything. *Did I even have a body anymore?* I was completely frozen.

Why did I hurt so much?

How did I get on the floor?

Where was my phone?

I need to get to the hospital.

I can't.

When I opened my eyes I saw my managers face in front of mine. His mouth was moving but his volume was muted. I couldn't hear anything apart from the pounding in my head and heart. After what felt like a spinning eternity, my ears started to depict words again. It sounded like I was underwater, completely drowning in its darkness.

"Jade? Calm down. What's happened?"

I couldn't talk. I opened my mouth but all my words just fell into sobs. I couldn't say the words… they weren't there, I could hear them in my head but my mouth wouldn't say them.

I felt sick to my core; my body didn't know whether it wanted to throw up or to shut down. I was removed from reality, I wasn't here anymore. In that moment, I felt my soul leave my body and ran as far away from me as possible (I don't think it's ever completely returned.)

I felt my eyes become darker. My face fell to no expression, my mouth closed and my lips lined parallel. My body went limp and I began to feel utterly paralysed.

In this moment, my reality changed. My life changed, and my soul changed. I changed.

"Babe what's happened? Talk to me, Jade? Is it your Mum?"

I heard the words and I responded in my mind but my mouth stayed shut. Instead my head jolted up and down. With that he knew, his face dropped and he stuttered: "babe, I'm so, so sorry. Let me get Cheryll" (my best friend.)

I couldn't physically feel the pain that was suffocating my chest. Mentally I knew it was there, it was tight and it completely ached. I just couldn't connect with the pain, I was numb.

My vision was blurred from the relentless tears in my eyes. They traced and fell from my face, only for my eyes to fill back up, a continuous circle.

I stared into complete nothingness, not focused on anything and nothing seemed to feature in my sight or mind. The first time ever, I actually had no thought process or vision. I was in a state of complete and utter emptiness. I was surrounded by everything but I felt nothing.

I don't recall how long Cheryll had been with me, I just remember hearing her for the first time, asking if I wanted any water. Hearing her voice and seeing her face, smacked a state of normality back into my existence.

"I need to go to the hospital. Can you get my stuff please?" This was all I could get out. With that Cheryll got my coat and I felt the uncomfortable emptiness creep back into my body. My mind returned to the empty darkness I had temporarily left.

My manager returned with Cheryll and requested that he drove me to the hospital. All I needed to do now was to walk out of that door and past everyone I worked with.

How the fuck can I do this?

Did they know?

Did they hear me?

Can they tell I've been crying?

Are my legs going to carry me that far?

I threw my head down and walked out, not looking back I just needed to get out. I needed to feel the fresh air on my skin. *I needed to feel something.*

I pushed open the door and walked out of the building. Instantly the fresh air smothered my skin (finally I felt something.) I was brought back to reality and I felt present in life again. I inhaled deeply and exhaled slowly, savouring every inch of the breath that left my lungs.

I pulled my phone out of my pocket, scrolled down my contact and pressed: Chloe. She was almost furniture in my family at this point; we had become good friends from working together. As the dial tone rang three times, I heard her say: "hey."

The words were there, but I couldn't speak. It was silent and the only sound was my breathing. Tears started to cradle my eyes once more.

How am I going to explain this?

"Jade, are you ok?"

"Erm, I can't, I'll text you." I managed to spit out, before hanging up. I couldn't say the words out loud, they were trapped. I opened my messages and typed the words instead. No emotion, no detail simply: *mum died.*

I got a reply instantly telling me she was on her way and that she would meet me at the hospital. I didn't even know if I wanted to be near anyone right now, I just had no energy or focus to try and figure it out. I simply replied ok.

Putting my phone back in my pocket, I swung open the door to my manager's car and I dropped down into the passenger seat. The anxiety built up throughout my body and I found myself feeling painfully numb once more.

Time had decided to manipulate my reality again. Every minute of the journey felt like hours. I couldn't speak and each time my manager made an attempt to converse, it fell into my ears and back out without any response.

Eventually the car came to a halt, and when I glanced up we were outside of the hospital. The pain that had wrapped around my heart, had dropped into the pit of my stomach and I felt the urge to be sick.

It was only the day before that I entered the same doors, and visited my mother who was happy, healthy and alive. Now I was looking at the same doors knowing her happiness had been stolen, her health was robbed from her and her life was taken away.

I managed to somehow get out the car and begin to approach the doors. I hadn't realised until I looked up but I was stood next to my brother. We never exchanged a single word; we simply walked side by side in heart breaking silence. Neither of us knew what to say but we understood the words we failed to share.

I felt tears stream down my cheeks every step of the way and the closer we got to the ward they got faster. We had passed twenty to thirty people that day; all witnessing my heart break whilst we walked towards our living nightmare. Although they saw us, in that moment I was alone and the corridors were lifeless.

Knowing I was going to see the woman who brought life to my body, air to my lungs, the beating to my heart, and the purpose to my existence, lying lifeless, on a hospital bed. Lungs empty of air, and a still heartbeat, made me want to be somebody else that day. I didn't want to be the person in that moment... in my moment.

What do I do when I get there?

What will she look like?

Will she still look like my Mum?

What do you say?

My mind was throwing questions back and forth, leaving me imprisoned in a panicked tennis match. I had never realised how annoying my inner voice was until it was asking stupid questions.

Myself and Jason eventually found our way to the ward and we waited numbly at the electronic doors. They slowly opened giving us entry to our new and unwanted reality. I felt my chest pull tighter, as if it was trying to cradle the shattered pieces of my heart and the tighter it got, the heavier my feet became. More tears fell from my eyes, burning my cheeks with each time. I gripped my hands together so tight; trying to calm the trembling shakes; that they turned white.

The nurse behind the reception desk instantly recognised me; she was the head nurse of the ward (the one mum had wrapped around her little finger, in less than 24 hours.) As I approached the desk, she walked towards me and for the first time that day, I felt a warmth crash into me and engulf my body. As I opened my eyes I was wrapped in her embrace. A moment of relief and security and for a split second I felt safe. It was short lived of course and when the nurse pulled her warmth away, my body regained its icy temperature.

"I'm so sorry for your loss. I'll take you to see her."

Wait. What? I Can't. I want to. I need to.

It'll be ok. No. I can't.

Whilst my inner voice argued with itself once more, I found myself drowning in my burning tears. "Darling, you don't have to if you don't want to." The nurse interjected the battle going on inside my mind.

Wait? Can she hear my thoughts? I hadn't said anything, well not out loud anyway... Inside my head was a different story.

How many voices were actually inside my head right now? Oh there's another one.

I was gasping for air and I needed to breathe but it felt like I was drowning... I opened my mouth and drew back a deep breath and when I exhaled, it felt as if I had pushed out my inner voice and replaced it with clarity and space.

"No, I want to. Just give me a moment." I calmly whispered.

I took in one more deep breath and nodded to the nurse, letting her know that I was ready. Obviously the reality was I wasn't really ready, when can you be? Can you ever be prepared to see your own mother lifeless? The answer is never; you can't prepare or be ready for that experience.

Jason and I moved aside allowing the nurse to lead the way, we approached a door and my heart beat relaxed. If I was going to do this, it needed to be in private with nobody else around. However the nurse walked past the door and once again I felt the panic and fear return. I wanted to hold onto that door handle and refuse to move.

Yesterday I had visited the same ward and looked into my mum's eyes. I watched her mouth move as she spoke and felt the light grip of her hand on mine. Today none of that would be possible: it wouldn't be possible today, tomorrow or ever again. This was it and with each step forward, the corridor seemed to expand further.

The nurse stopped and placed her hands behind her, she twisted her feet so that she was facing us. Her head slowly and gently bowed down before lifting straight back up. Despite visiting this same ward every day since mum was admitted, it felt unknown, alien and uncomfortable.

I glanced around and saw all the open cubicles, with the patients wide eyed and silent. You could taste the sympathy and it tasted vile, I hated it. They shouldn't have had to look at us with any sympathy. *Don't feel sorry for me because this shouldn't be happening. I shouldn't be standing waiting to say goodbye to my mother's lifeless shell.*

Mum's cubical stood out illuminated by the blue curtains hiding my worst nightmare. I followed Jason as he ripped open a gap in the curtains to expose an entrance, my feet carried me unconsciously in behind him. I didn't think it was possible to hurt any more, cry any harder than I already had, and break any further than I already was. I was overflowing with emptiness.

The image my eyes were massacred with will haunt me for the rest of my life. It's hard to explain the wounding you feel; when you're faced with the final time you'll be able to see someone. Words fail you especially when the love for that person is unconditional.

My eyes captured the cold, sad and empty image of mum lying unresponsive in her bed. They then diverted to my usually intimidating, bulky, strong and protective dad. Except, the image I saw was a man who was exposed, face soaked with tears and his body was crowded by the chair he sat in.

I heard the very similar screams that invaded my ears earlier but this time, the screams were filled with much more raw and aching agony. Each scream that landed cut me deeper than if my skin was sliced open with a blade. I was once again throwing my pain out of my mouth. I had lost my control once again and I was sobbing. I fell into my dad's arms and found peace, crying heavily into his neck. His arms held me securely and he managed to sooth me out of my sobs. I was left silently jolting back broken cries with gasps of air in between.

I reluctantly pulled away from my dad's protection, placing myself on mums' cold and absent bedside. I placed her tiny, stone cold and limp hand into mine. I desperately wanted my warmth to awaken her and hold my hand but it didn't happen. It didn't stop me from trying; I rubbed my thumb back and forth over her hand, which was now catching my falling tears too.

Her face was so still as if it was locked into a position she was unable to break free from. However it was a position she didn't seem to want to break free from. She looked so perfectly peaceful, her face was so relaxed and her body was flaccid. It was a disturbingly beautiful reality. This was the only time in my life I saw my mother with no pain, no stress and no worries. She finally looked free.

My brother stood at the foot of her bed: unable to move, unable to speak and unable to cry (to be honest I had to keep on checking he was still there.) In that moment his silence, coldness and inability to act were the hardest things to stomach. I could feel his heart breaking, his silence spoke volumes. He didn't know what to do and that is the epitome of losing a loved one. You're completely lost and at a loss. You don't only lose that person; you lose your reality, your normality, and a part of your world. You lose a part of your life and even worse, you lose yourself.

Author's Note:

It took so long to write this chapter. The first time since I started writing this book, I genuinely thought I couldn't do it. I believed I wouldn't be able to finish it. I've tried to be the rawest I can emotionally be. This chapter in particular, took two weeks to finish. I had to stop several times because I couldn't see the screen through my tears. It will never matter how much time passes, this will always rip my heart open. Sometimes it scares me talking about, in fear I'll slip back to the depths of my darkness. I wanted to tell you guys this as, I feel you're reading parts of my life and when writing this chapter, I gained another experience. One I truly didn't expect or even know how to handle at first.

Chapter Ten: D.N.R Part II

I stayed at mum's bedside, still gripping her progressively cold hand in mine. As you know her hands were always cold: she was always cold in fact, but this time it was different. It wasn't different because she was no longer living; it was the way it felt. The way it felt in my heart, her coldness had travelled to my heart.

Her hands radiated a chilling touch and they weighed more than ever. They didn't feel like hands anymore, especially the hands of my mother. The hands I would always hold, and have to rub between my palms to try and warm up, were no longer present.

Even though I knew she was gone, I still found myself instinctively trying to warm her hands. I attempted to circulate the heat from my hands to hers, trying not to be too rough because of her arthritis. Nothing happened of course, my warmth was rejected and her hands grew a shade darker (I didn't want to accept that right now in this new world, she felt nothing.)

After realising that I couldn't warm her hands up; I bit down on my lip trapping my heartbreak that wanted to scream out. I raised her hand to my lips and pressed a light kiss on the back of it. The more I thought about: how different her touch was, how motionless she was, how deeply mauve her lips were growing, the more it dawned on me that she was no longer here. Her body was the only thing left but it was simply the shell she was once protected by. My mum, my mama bear was no longer here. She had gone. All that remained was a deceased body imitating what she once looked like.

No words were exchanged between me, dad or Jason and our silence was deafeningly loud. *I mean what is there to be said?* We were hurting way more than we had before. Our faces grew longer, paler, emptier and our eyes sunk in the depths of the darkness surrounding us. Our hearts were reluctantly beating, scared in case more pieces fell off. I have no recollection or even the slightest memory of time on that day. I couldn't tell you if I had been at the hospital for minutes, hours, days, months or even years.

When I've been faced with difficulties in life: like mum being diagnosed with cancer, time had always tricked me. It made me feel as if substantial amounts had passed when in reality; hardly any had passed at all. This time round though, it hadn't tricked me. It didn't feel like a minute was an hour or vice versa, it just stood still. Time didn't exist, its concept was foreign and it wasn't yet invented to me. I felt like an alien in life. My mind was distant, my body was numb and my heart was cold. I didn't feel alive and I felt like I was a witness to something happening around me, not something happing *to* me.

I stared unconsciously at the face that was once my mothers, it was lying lifeless and heavily on the pillow. My mind was spinning around in my head, surrendering to the crippling hollowness. The only way I can explain how it felt, is imagine a vinyl record spinning around constantly. No sound transmitting and no art work showing, simply a blank, black empty disc spinning with no purpose or reason. That's exactly how I felt.

The single streaks of hot tears falling down my face threw me back into reality. Each time I wiped my cheeks, I hoped the stinging and burning pain would be soothed, but instead it felt like sandpaper had replaced my hands. All I felt that day was pain, it came in every direction, just pure unforgiving pain.

It was painful to cry and my eyes burned every time I blinked. My eyelids felt like they had been replaced with broken glass. My cheeks felt scorched and cut, stinging as if I had paper cuts across them. My throat scratched with every gulp, becoming drier each time I swallowed. My head felt like elephants were stampeding back and forth. My whole body ached as if I had been pummelled by a heavy weight boxer.

The worst pain I felt that day was the pain inside my chest… in my heart. It didn't only ache but it hurt, it physically hurt. It was sharp and with every breath I took, I felt a stabbing in my chest. I have never felt intense pain like that before. I believe that heart break is not a state of mind; true heart break is a physical pain.

Sadistically I didn't want the pain to end. I needed to feel something because the numbness was suffocating me. The way each nerve ending in my body felt unbearable pain was refreshing because it reminded me I was still alive (which really was a double edged sword.) I was alive and breathing like I was the day before and the day before that. Except on this day, I was now alive in a world where my mum no longer was.

After unknown amounts of time more of us were around mum's bedside. Each new face was harder to handle. Just when I felt myself calming down someone new would enter and their emotions wiped me back off my feet, engulfing me in a tsunami of pain. Not everyone who came to pay their respects stayed (I mean I don't blame them one bit.) The sight was horrific; each minute that went by she was less and less of the person we knew.

Some of the day is still a blur, there are probably more details than I've given, but I have suppressed them so far into my subconscious they're oblivious to me. One of the hardest, gut wrenching and heart shattering moments from that day (aside from the fact my mother had died,) was the moment my sister and my nephew Harry arrived. As I've said, Harry was the apple of mum's eye. He lived with us for the majority of his childhood. He adored mum as much as she adored him, he was a nanny's boy. At the age of eighteen he had experienced his first loss and the biggest to him. The lady who helped shape his childhood, cooked, cleaned and cared unconditionally for him.

I heard Kelly whispering from behind the curtain and my heart dropped to the pit of my stomach, because I knew that Harry was with her. I tried to anticipate Harry's reaction, I knew I was about to watch his face take in the image of his Nan for the last time. When the curtains ruffled I took in a quick breath and closed my eyes simultaneously. I wanted to hide from my reality and pretend none of this had happened. As my eyes lifted open, I released the air I was holding onto and I saw my sister walk through the gap in the curtains. Harry followed behind with his head down and his eyes fixed to the floor beneath his feet. I didn't want him to look up, he wasn't ready for this (I wasn't ready for this.)

Kelly managed to shield the view of mum for a moment, until she sat down on the bed next to her. The sight of mum was now exposed and Harry's eyes widened as they took in his nan, for the final time in his life. His body trembled and gravity left him stranded but before his legs buckled bellow him, he was caught from hitting the floor.

I stood frozen on the spot, every fibre in my body wanted to run to him. In my mind I had already caught him but in reality I hadn't moved. The only movement from my body was the tears pouring down my face, and I couldn't breathe. I felt suffocated.

Why did this happen? This wasn't fair! Why her? Why us? What was we being punished for?

Harry's reaction had got us all in the middle, to the left, right, top and bottom of our already obliterated hearts again. Dad was biting hard on his lip trying not to scream out, Jason couldn't look and had to turn away and Kelly was crying beside mum (wanting nothing more than to be comforted by the one person who no longer could.)

Harry somehow had calmed down and he slowly made his way over to the right of mum's bed, gently placing his hand over hers. What he said next... none of us could handle. Still to this day, I don't understand how we all survived the continuous heart break in one day.

"Grandad she's so cold, she doesn't like being cold. Can't they make her a hot water bottle?" Harry struggled to hold back his cries, his words had hit his own ears and punched their way to his innocent heart. Dad couldn't take anymore and had to leave, he asked if Harry wanted to go with him to get some air and thankfully he did. I couldn't watch his shattering heart play out and not being able to do a thing about it.

I had become totally accustomed to, or just oblivious to, the fact we were not just sharing the worst day of our lives together, but we were sharing it with everyone else present in that ward that day too. The curtains may have hidden the visual heartbreak, but they certainly didn't silence any of it. It only snapped into my consciousness when our silence was invaded by a doctor talking to another patient.

It made me feel desperately uncomfortable and unbelievably exposed. Although I didn't have much conception of time, I knew for a fact that we must have been in the cubical with mum for hours. Meaning, for hours these strangers were surrounded by our screams, our conversations and our echoing silences. Not only was this uncomfortable for us, it must have been horrific for those around us, prisoned by their own health worries and my families grief.

"Now I have to check, you're happy for us to jump on your chest if we need to?" That was what we heard next to us and it was the last punch we took. Chloe, whose presence I had completely neglected without meaning to, walked out and only returned moments later with the head nurse. "Guys, I'm sorry. We've sorted out a room. If you guys could follow me I'll take you there and mum will be brought in shortly."

Finally we had space and privacy as a family and ironically now that we all had the freedom and privacy to cry and scream, none of us could. It was like the room had silenced our heartbreak. I hate myself for ever feeling this but the longer I spent around mum's body, the more I just wanted to leave and go home.

The body lying in front of me was not my mum; it was cold, still and dead. My mother was no longer here, she wasn't the person we were saying our goodbyes to. It was simply a replica of the woman I had visited yesterday. For starters, she would have hated us all staring at her and she certainly would have moaned about how cold she was.

There were more of us now than there was in the cubical. Sitting around the body lying in front of us was me, Dad, Jason, Kelly, Harry, Chloe and mum's sister Patsy and my Cousin Jo (mum really would have despised this.) As we became accustom to our new surroundings, a nurse knocked on the door before entering and wheeled in a trolley stocked with four white tea pots and numerous cups.

"I thought you guys may want tea and coffee."

Wait…What the…?

We were sitting around my mother's deceased body, *why would we want to have a cup of tea?*

These questions simply swam around my head instead of saying what I was really thinking. In true British fashion we all thanked her and welcomed the unusual sentiment (all of us sharing equal levels of confusion.)

As confusing as the gesture was, what leaves me more baffled is: it actually had an impact on us. Firstly we all probably needed some sort hydration, but for some reason it made us talk about things. Things like: what mum used to say, what she would do and for the very first time that day we were told what had happened that morning.

We started sharing anecdotes; all of us smiling and at times releasing small laughs (I had forgotten I was capable of laughing.) I forgot that my voice could produce anything other than painful cries. I had forgotten that my mind could project happiness. I had forgotten what that warm feeling felt like when I was happy. It felt nice, it felt alien in consideration of my surroundings but it felt so nice.

The thing about grief, is that it makes you feel every single emotion: one's you never realised you had. It makes you feel each one all at the same time. Its relentless, it's narcissistic and merciless. You might get a snippet of happiness but it gets ripped apart by guilt. Grief hits you immediately and it doesn't wait for you to catch up. It takes over and it can quickly possess you.

I would smile and laugh along with everyone else in the room, and then instantly I was attacked by guilt. I felt ashamed to be expressing the happiness the memories gave me.

Why are you happy? What are you smiling for? Your mother's dead, how can you smile? (There were those voices again.)

Then reality pinned me down and reminded me that I was smiling and laughing at a memory. I would never, ever be able to create more. All the ones I smiled at will be the only ones I will ever have.

How messed up is that?

I apologise at not being able to recall who asked but someone asked the question. The question I guess we all wanted to know but no one wanted to hear or ask.

"So, what happened? Was she in pain?"

One thing for sure, no tea or coffee in the world would make this a good memory.

We all looked towards dad who cleared his throat…

"No, she didn't suffer and she wasn't in pain. In fact, it was quick and you can see in her face, she didn't feel anything. Erm, I got here about 7:45am, she kicked off because I was 15 minutes late (small smirks lined on our faces, imagining it.) Anyway, I washed her and got her dressed and back in bed. Then we were just talking and she just told me, she couldn't breathe. With that I called for the nurse. They put the oxygen mask over her face and she seemed a bit better. The nurse left and then she took the mask back off and said it wasn't helping and that she still couldn't breathe. I did no more and called for the nurse again. They came in and swapped it for the tubes up the nose. Well with that as I looked down, her eyes started to roll back and the nurse smashed the button for help. As they all come running in, I was taken to the waiting room. I was sat there for 10 minutes, so I went to get a nurse to find out what was happening and I knew straight away, that was it. I just told her to stop, no more and to let her go, she doesn't want to be resuscitated, she has a DNR."

We all fell silent, none of us wanting to be the first one to say a word.

"I'm just glad she didn't suffer, it was quick and she wasn't in pain." Dad said before knocking back what remained in his cup.

I didn't know what to say, so I didn't say a word, I remained silent.

Did it make me feel better knowing how it happened?

Absolutely and categorically not, it didn't change the fact she's gone. However it did release the worry of thinking about her suffering before she passed but no… I never felt better.

Why did she have a DNR?

Mum decided when the time came, she wanted to just go. I think her seeing her own mother being supported by machines helping her breathe made it easier to make the decision. Her mentality was when it's your time, why fight it? She had spent too much of her life fighting and she had, had enough of it.

Did I wish I was there?

Each and every single day I regret not being there. I will always have to live with not being one of the last people she spoke to. I wasn't one of the last people she smiled at and one of the last she said goodbye to. Of course it wouldn't have changed what happened but at least I could have just been there. Instead I was at work, oblivious to my mother's last breath. I will always struggle to accept that.

I'd had enough of being in that cold, clinical, smothering and depressing room. I'd had enough of sitting, looking at the lifeless, coldly blue body choosing to pose as my mother and I wanted to go home. Regardless of how long we stayed with the body, mum was never going to come home with us. As emotionless as is sounds, we were just surrounding a body of nothingness. It had no warmth, no expression and no life and it was just disturbingly morbid now.

"Can we go home now please? It's not mum anymore." I carefully whispered to dad who simply agreed and then softly announced to everyone that we were leaving. He reminded everyone how much mum hated people gawking at her and one by one, we all got up, said our final goodbyes and left. I think I was the only one who didn't plant a goodbye kiss on her. I couldn't handle the feeling of her frozen and distant skin on my lips one more time.

As me and dad thanked the nurses for all they had done, the head nurse came towards us. Her face wore a small, sympathetic yet welcomed smile before placing me and dad into separate hugs.

"I'm so sorry again for your loss. Your mother was an angel, and she was my favourite patient. Whatever she wanted she got. Never before have I had to leave the ward because of the death of a patient, until today. I had to be taken into a room because I couldn't stop crying. Your mother and wife was a very special lady."

I appreciated her words more than anything that day. This was a complete stranger sharing our mourning. I'm normally a really sceptical person but her words felt sincere and to be honest, I couldn't care less if they weren't. If she tells everyone in that situation, that same thing, I'd be quite happy because it made me feel a sense of warmth on one of the coldest days.

We said our final thank you's and walked to the exit. I wanted nothing more than to be at home and I almost felt happy about it, until grief decided to jump on my shoulders. For the last few hours, every part of me wanted and needed to be at home. Yet now I'm questioning if I was actually ready.

Why do you want to go home? She won't be there. Will it even feel like home anymore? What are you going to do exactly at home? She won't be there you know, she's gone. (These voices were really getting on my nerves.)

Chapter Eleven – Wide Awake

How can something that has been a part of your life now feel so odd? How can something so natural, normal and familiar, now feel so new?

I stood facing my front door, the same one I used daily to go in and out of my home. Yet it stood before me, completely foreign and unknown. It didn't feel like my home, the home I lived in…it was different. The feeling of distance and unfamiliarity grew stronger when I walked into the living room. This was a room that was once filled with light, warmth, love and company.

This room was the heart of our home, it was where we sat, watched television, ate dinner, talked, laughed and argued together. Where every Christmas was celebrated, presents wrapped and unwrapped, where love was shared and conversations had. Now it felt so far away from that and it no longer felt like the living room I had once loved. In fact, the longer I stood there the more of me died inside.

Darkness was the only greeting we had when we first stepped through the door. It brutally reminded us that nobody was there. The emptiness of it ran circles around us and it made me feel overwhelmingly lonely. There was no warmth; it felt like I had walked into a fridge. The cold tugged at my hands trying to walk me further into its core. I felt like an unwanted guest in someone else's home. The place I had lived for all of my life had become merely bricks and mortar.

Despite feeling like a stranger in my own home, I was still relieved that I was no longer in a hospital room, watching over my mother's dead body. Yet in the hospital I was with mum, I was around her and now I was without her. She would never be home again, at least not physically.

I couldn't catch a break. *Where was it better to be? At the hospital with my mother's dead body or at home that now felt overcrowded with loneliness?*

Everyone came back to our house after the hospital but when they left, the suffocating loneliness had pounded its way through me once again. I was intoxicated in my own thoughts with sadness drowning me in its unforgiving river. *Was this really happening? Was this it?*

Dad went upstairs to make some phone calls and that's when I truly felt it. I was sat on the sofa completely swamped with space and silence. I was slowly losing every part of the person I was yesterday. I felt my whole existence change; I was simply becoming a volt of deep confusion and emotions.

I was soon rushed back to reality when I heard a knock on the front door. I was half tempted to ignore it and let whoever it was continue knocking until they gave up. Yet here I was reaching for the handle, pulling it down releasing the security it gave. Standing in front of me was my neighbour who lived across from us. I dreaded what he had to say and having to respond made me feel physically sick.

"How is she?"

Fantastic! He doesn't know? I haven't had to say the words out loud all today. I haven't had to explain a single thing to anyone. Now I find myself staring into the eyes of my neighbour, who doesn't know what had happened. I have to answer the question of how my dead mother was. *I mean, can I just say it like that?* "Oh mum… Erm, wel,l not doing ok, in fact she's dead."

It sounds cold and obnoxious to be angry at someone who had done nothing wrong but I wasn't angry at my neighbour. I was angry with the inability to function, the inability to structure the words together and I was angry with the situation. Actually I was more than angry; I was broken-hearted, aching, hurting and invisibly bleeding.

I couldn't find any words, I just stared into his eyes, practically into his soul. He instinctively knew something horrific had happened, probably from my loss of human functions. I couldn't answer a simple question.

Thankfully dad came down from upstairs, saving me from wanting to smash down onto my knees and curl into a hysterical ball. I span my head around and just whispered in a broken voice: "it's Darren." Dad exchanged places with me, and I took the opportunity to fall onto the sofa, trying desperately not to cry.

I heard the destruction the news had on our neighbour. He adored mum and she adored him too. A small yet painful cry at the disbelief she had gone. I heard small distant sounds of slapping skin and it made me curious. When I peered out of the window my dad was being embraced. Two stocky, heavily built, physically intimidating looking grown men, consoling each other. *How was this fair?*

After dad came back inside: he had a bath it had been a long day for him. I mean it was a long day for all of us but for him, he had experienced the whole thing. Once he went into the bathroom, I found myself being swallowed up by the loneliness and sorrow once more.

My heart and body felt empty but my mind was occupied by an excruciating headache. It blasted through every inch of my head making it feel too heavy for my shoulders. I needed to rest so I pulled down the cushion on the sofa, and placed my head down. Finally I was lying down.

I closed my eyes in the hopes I got lost in a peaceful sleep. I just wanted to sleep and then wake back up and realise it was a horrible dream. I couldn't handle being conscious in this hellish reality any longer: in *my* hellish reality.

Did I sleep?

Nope… not one wink of sleep. The harder I tried to convince myself to sleep, the more awake I became. The closest to being asleep was closing my eyes. My eyes were shut but my mind was wide open, free and roaming through all of the events of the day. Mums face, her body, the phone call, the missed calls, the car ride, Harry, my dad, Jason, her face, her body and back around again. My mind was literally stuck on a horrific showreel loop, torturing me with each scene. I just wanted it to stop; I needed it to stop and to give me a break. All I wanted was a moment's peace, without being reminded that I had lost my mother. I wanted the pain in my heart, the pain in my head and everywhere else to stop.

A warm tear ran down the temple of my head and I heard myself softly whisper into the air: "please just stop, please just stop." I don't know what or who I was begging with but I needed something, someone, anyone and anything to hear me and to help.

However nothing stopped and everything still hurt, it still ached, and it continued to break further. To add more discomfort to my headache, my dog was barking continuously. I tried to plea for her to stop, but she just simply ignored me. Without a second thought I grabbed the cushion that was under my head, and I threw it in the direction the bark was echoing from. Refusing to open my eyes, I hoped that the direction was correct.

A smashing noise bolted me up from my position. The cushion had wiped out one of mum's crystal ornaments that were on the middle of the coffee table. Unfortunately the ornament took the full impact of my frustration.

What else can be destroyed today? I was so annoyed with myself. I shouldn't have thrown the cushion. If I hadn't had thrown it, I wouldn't be picking up the shattered pieces of crystal from the floor...Nothing much else happened that evening (nothing that is still within memory that is. I struggled to remember aspects of the day when writing this chapter. It was like piecing together a scrap book and all the pieces were cut out roughly with no order.)

The last thing I remember from that day was finally lying in my bed, surrounded by the darkness and the stillness of my room. Normally I can't sleep if there's the slightest bit of light; I have to be in complete darkness accompanied with deafening silence too. Only then am I ever able to fall asleep. However, this night was an exception, the darkness felt overwhelming, it was smothering. I felt uncomfortable, irritated and lonely.

The quiet and stillness of my room was louder than anything I've heard. The silence screamed at me making me feel the loneliness in my heart harder. I spent the whole night staring into absolute nothingness, just vacuumed inside my head with my thoughts for company. I felt the pressing need to run away, I don't know where I wanted to run to, and I don't know why I wanted to run, I just wanted to run and run until I couldn't anymore. I wanted to be somewhere it didn't hurt.

I was exhausted, my eyes felt like weights as they continued to fight against sleep. My head was still being force-fed the day's showreel. My heart ached under my chest and sent rivers of pain through my body. All I wanted and needed was some sleep; I wanted to drift into a state of unconsciousness and to get lost into a new reality, where none of this was true. It didn't happen and instead I spent the whole entire night wide awake, hiding under the blanket of darkness my eyelids had created.

The whole night was a mixture of either being paralyzed and unable to move or irritated and uncomfortably tossing and turning. One minute I'd be lying motionlessly fixated on the emptiness, with the deafening silence terrorising my conscious. Then I'd be fighting against the comfort of my bed, throwing my body into different positions. My mind didn't stop racing through thought after thought and memory after memory. The one thought that stood out louder than any other (and still to this day it makes me shudder,) was the thought of my dad.

I had always slept alone in my double bed and my room had always been silent. There was nobody lying next to me when I rolled over. Dad on the other hand had shared his bed and his space for over twenty years with someone. Now he was surrounded by an empty space, if he rolled over no one would be there. If it was too cold there wasn't another person for warmth. Unlike the last twenty years, mum wasn't there and her side was occupied by her absence.

I was smothered in pain in my bed but I couldn't imagine the pain my dad felt. A part of me wanted to go in and just lie with him but I couldn't bring myself to move. Instead I kept thinking about him lying alone, hurting and cold. I was trapped in my thoughts and there was nothing I could do to stop them.

My room began to slowly fill with light that crept through the window. It was no longer night time and I had not had a second of sleep. I had to accept the tiredness my body felt and get up to face the day. With the lack of sleep my head was pounding with pain, it thumped and it throbbed. Each time I moved it only got worse. I reached for my phone and pressed down the home button, the time was: 4:00AM.

The last time I had looked at the time was at 10:00am the previous day, as this was when I called the briefing at work. The briefing before my life shattered around me without mercy. I continued to check the time on my phone, until I saw it hit 8:00am. I had already heard dad get up way before that but decided to stay put. If I'm honest I didn't want to speak, see or be around anyone. Nevertheless the pain in my head at this point, felt like my skull was splitting open. I had no other option but to get up because I needed painkillers.

It felt even more alien when I walked into the living room as I expected mum to be sitting on the sofa drinking her tea. It wasn't because I had forgotten what had happened; it just felt confusing and sad that she wasn't there.

After losing someone you love; aside from the unbelievable agony you feel, you really are submerged into a state of confusion. You struggle to comprehend the simplest things and nothing makes sense. I guess it's a result of your previous normality fighting against the newest adjustment of your normal. The normal routines and all the things you used to do get sent to autopilot. It's like nothing has changed, expect everything has changed. You become stuck in a state of limbo and it's disturbingly natural.

The morning after mum had died was my first experience of being in a limbo state of mind. I walked into the living room and was expecting mum to be there. I wasn't the only one; dad also had a slap of limbo that morning too. Making his usual morning coffee, which was a habit now felt like the worst decision he had made.

When my eyes met his face I noticed the colour had drained from his skin. His face was grey and ridden of any life, I was apprehensive in asking what was wrong. Another abnormal feeling attached to something that would have been normally natural to do but thankfully he spoke before I did. "I made myself a coffee this morning, wasn't until I finished I realised I made mum a tea too." That was all that was said, but I couldn't respond, nothing I could have said would have helped. There are no words that can comfort you when you're adjusting to the death of someone you loved unconditionally. Therefore we sat in silence both knowing and understanding exactly how the other was feeling.

In only twenty four hours my life had been turned upside down and my normality was twisted beyond repair. Every part of my reality had now become unfamiliar territory. I normally hate the cliché sayings like: 'world turned upside down' but it was the closest description of how it felt. One day previous everything was in place and gravity held things down, and people were where they were supposed to be. Fast forward twenty four hours, everything slid down around me and nothing was in place. No matter how tight I tried to hold on, I was losing grip and I was wide awake in a living nightmare.

The rest of the day was tainted with the same limbo feeling. Every Saturday dad would go into town and do the food shopping, put a couple of bets on and have breakfast. Out of complete habit, that is exactly what he did. I decided that I would go with him, fuelled by the fear of being alone with just my mind as company. I found myself in familiar territory, doing the normal things I had always done. My body was behaving normally but my brain knew it wasn't right. It wasn't familiar, the world and everything around me was moving just like it normally would. However my whole life had just changed, nothing was normal, everything that was once familiar was now unfamiliar and unnatural.

Still to this day, on my bad days these feelings come back and the most simplistic things can seem completely unnatural. That's the ugliness of grief, it doesn't have a specific date and time it starts and it certainly doesn't have an expiry date.

There is never a time when things feel the same as they used to.

There isn't a single minute in the day, where I don't find myself

thinking about my mother. All the things she would have said and

done in situations. I constantly find myself thinking about the: 'what

ifs.' It never brings any comfort; actually the 'if's' hurt more

because, they remind you that they will never be possible.

Chapter Twelve – No One To Wear Black

One thing is certain: you should never underestimate the resilience of the human body. It adapts very quickly to circumstance and situations. Even in the depths of pain and trauma, the human body and mind can switch into auto pilot and get things done.

Still the last thing you want to do whilst, you're emotionally exposed is to plan and organise a funeral. To plan and organise the final goodbye for the person whose passing, is the reason your chest feels ripped open, is devastating. Yet the magnitude of it becomes surprisingly manageable and before you know it, a date is set, a place of service and three songs have been selected to play on the day.

For anyone who has had to do this, from the bottom of my heart you have every ounce of my respect and empathy. For those who are going through this right now, you have my unconditional admiration and understanding. Lastly, for those who haven't had to do this yet, you have every ounce of my non-judgemental envy.

Planning my mother's funeral whilst I was still mourning her life was one of the hardest things I've had to do. At the age of twenty five, I hadn't done a great deal of funeral planning, so, I didn't know where to start. *I mean, how do invitations work? Do I send invitations through the post? Is a text message better? Is a Facebook post easier? Wait...are you even invited to funerals?*

I didn't have the slightest idea of what needed to be done or what I needed to do first. All I knew was some of mum's wishes. In the least morbid sense, mum would sometimes discuss particular things she wanted if she died. Although that may sound extremely dark, the conversations were not random. We never had these discussions over Sunday dinner ("can you pass the gravy, oh speaking of passing, when I die I want...") thankfully it was never like that, because that would have totally spoilt the ambiance of a family Sunday lunch.

Mum hated people wearing black to a funeral, she believed funerals were already sad enough. Therefore she told us when her time comes, that no one is to wear typical funeral clothes. They were to attend wearing their comfortable clothes and as much colour as they liked.

"I want it to be as cheap as you can get it," was another request. We were reminded of this each time the topic came up. Mum didn't want bells and whistles either; she wanted it to be as cheap as possible and over quickly.

In fact I recall one conversation we had together. Mum told me that she doesn't want us to skint ourselves because she wouldn't be around to benefit from it. The funny thing is despite it sounding rude as hell, I actually think she had the right idea. I mean nobody goes to a funeral to critique how expensive it looks (if you do you're an idiot.)

The one request she had that did help us in the planning was the type of service she wanted. Mum made it abundantly clear that she wanted to have a cremation service and not a burial. She said about the upkeep and constant maintenance a grave took, and she didn't want us to have that worry. Another reason she wanted to be cremated was because she didn't want to be eaten by worms.

When I thought back to those conversations (despite them being morbid,) they made me smile. I felt a weird sense of happiness, granted they aren't the normal memories which spark happiness. I felt happy because I finally remembered the sound of her voice. I remembered her characteristics, her sense of humour, her silliness, her bluntness and more importantly, I remembered her.

From the Friday she died until the moment we had to think about the funeral plans, I couldn't picture her before she went into hospital. Anytime I saw her in my thoughts, she was lying in that hospital bed. The thoughts had no sound, it was like everything had been muted and I couldn't hear her voice. It terrified me not only had she physically gone, but she had been erased from my memories too. I felt like I had lost her completely. So when I heard her voice talking to me through those memories, I smiled because she came back and I had a piece of her with me. My happiness was short lived as the reality of what I was planning, and the conversations I was remembering brought me back to earth. Once again my heart was stabbed with life's double edged sword.

Dad and I had planned to register her death and make the funeral arrangements on the same day. We just wanted to get it done in one clean sweep. We knew that both of the tasks were going to be an emotional overload for us, so there was no sense in repeating the trauma. Plus the lack of sleep that was affecting us both wouldn't have gotten us through.

I managed to get some sleep on the Sunday after she died: a total of twelve hours to be exact. I was so relieved and grateful that my body and mind allowed itself a chance to rest. It was the first time since mum had died that I had fallen into a deep sleep, it was more than I was used to but less than I needed. However, it didn't happen without some help.

On the Sunday I received a text from Cheryll asking if I wanted to go and see her. It was a chance to get out of the house and have a change of scenery and I needed that. However, I had not slept for two nights and I was utterly exhausted. A part of me was tempted to put it off and continue to wallow myself in pity, but I didn't.

When I got to Cheryll's, she made me a tea and offered to make me food but I declined, I didn't really have an appetite. At this point my headache had really intensified and I needed to ease the pain. It started to make me feel sick so I asked for some painkillers. Cheryll had recently had an operation and only had Codeine in the house. Without thinking I took one, I just wanted this headache gone but I didn't know how strong those tablets were. Within half an hour I was sleeping in her fully reclined arm chair. I woke up disorientated and had no idea where I was (wow those tablets were good.) This was the first time in 48 hours I had managed to sleep. I still felt unbelievably tired though but as for the headache, it was gone and I was feeling as close to normal as I had in a while.

I was struggling to keep my eyes open so I decided to head back home. I couldn't wait to get home and just lie down; thankfully it's only a five minute walk back home. When I got back my brother was there talking with dad in the living room. I could feel my eyes closing for longer each time I blinked. I fought against the urge to sleep for another hour but I couldn't hold out any longer. I laid down on the floor in the living room and the next thing I remember, dad woke me up and told me to go up to bed. I had fallen into such a deep sleep that when I stood up, my whole body was numb.

I had now managed to get a total of an hour's sleep, it was a feeling that I had missed for the last two days. I missed having to wipe the sleep from my eyes, stretching the night's relaxation from my muscles. I missed the feeling of not knowing where the hell you were when you first wake up. I even missed trying to tame the bed hair in the morning.

I climbed into my bed, sunk my head onto my pillow and hid my body under my duvet. I'd forgotten how it felt, not remembering falling asleep. It was a feeling that came back to me the next morning though. I had slept for 11 straight hours and I didn't have any memory of the night. I had no nightmares, no dreams, no tossing or turning, just undisturbed rest. I even woke up in the position I got into bed in. I was hung-over on sleep, my eyes felt heavy, my body was stiff and my head was empty…it felt so good.

As small as it sounds: I felt like some things were finally going back to a place of normality. I was once again able to close my eyes and have a nights rest; I had finally got sleep back. Not everything was back to normal of course. After all, there was one thing that would never be normal; I no longer had a mother but having the ability to sleep again, felt like a small win for me in a game full of losses.

All the days had seemingly rolled into one and before we knew it we needed to begin the proceedings of mum's cremation (along with all the other essential tasks.) Neither myself, nor dad had work the week after mum passed away so we decided to do everything that week. First task on our agenda was to collect mum's medical certificate from the hospital. We needed the certificate to register the death, which we needed to plan the funeral. You see these are the small things that I had no idea about. I never knew that someone dying was such an administrative assignment.

The medical certificate also showed us what the cause of death was. I felt a surge of anxiety knowing I was going to see what caused her to die. *Was it something that could have been avoided? Would it be something that just happens or was it uncommon?* I had question after question spinning around my head because I couldn't find an answer to them.

We had decided to take chocolates to the nurses who looked after mum as we were back at the hospital. Knowing I would be walking back into the same ward where I last saw my mother; both alive and deceased made my body tense in anxiety and fear. Arriving at the hospital my heart crumbled with confusion, it didn't know whether to beat faster or stop beating all together. The closer we got to the entrance the more present it's beating inside my chest became. My knees mirrored my hearts confusion, unable to decide whether to carry me inside or buckle beneath me. My hands were discretely trembling inside my coat pockets, increasing in temperature and collecting sweat in every crease. The dryness of my mouth grew at speed. It felt as if I had been sucking on sand for a week. My throat was playing a game of hot potato with the lump that had invaded my airways. Whilst every part of my anatomy fought against itself, I found myself walking towards the all too familiar electronic doors of the ward, which held the memories of my living nightmare.

My feet carried me to the nurse's desk, an all too familiar situation which I found myself in, only days previous. It was just this time around, I wasn't in any receipt of bad news. I don't know what felt worse? The fact that days before, I was in the same ward saying goodbye to my already lifeless mother, or the fact that I was in the same ward where I kissed mum goodnight after spending hours talking, laughing and just living. This ward was the last place I saw my mother alive but even worse it was the last time I got to see her in my lifetime.

I was holding a box of chocolates, facing the same nurse who comforted me on the day and, it broke my heart into a million pieces all over again. *This really did happen.* This was the first taste of reality I had experienced since she passed. The numbness and the denial had now been replaced with deep sadness.

This really was it. It had finally hit me that I would never see her ever again. I would never speak to her again and hear her voice. I would never be able to feel her touch and I would never be able to create new memories with her. This was it, she was actually gone. I was so deeply rooted in denial that I had hoped it was all a massive misunderstanding. I had hoped that we would get a phone call to say they got it wrong. We would go to see her and she would be lying in bed and this would be just an incredibly unfortunate mistake.

It wasn't reality and it wasn't true, it was all just hope and delusion. There were no mistakes and no misunderstandings, she had passed away and she wasn't coming back. I wasn't going to be sitting next to her bedside talking to her because my mum was undeniably gone. It took every ounce of strength that I had left in my broken body, not to fall to the floor and cry my sadness away once more.

I still don't know how I held it together, how I never allowed a tear to fall is beyond me. I almost choked on the lump that had taken up residence in my throat. The tears built up and quite honestly I really wanted to cry, it just didn't happen. I couldn't let go of the emotions tearing me apart inside, *maybe it was my way of trying to hold onto something of her.* After all...I just had the biggest reality check she wasn't coming back, ever.

We exchanged hugs with the head nurse and I handed over the box of chocolates. Dad took the lead and gave our gratitude and appreciation for all they did for mum.

"I'm truly sorry for your loss."

I'm truly sorry for your loss, I'm truly sorry for your loss, I'm truly sorry for your loss. That one sentence summersaulted over and over in my head. My ears hearing it louder each time my mind repeated it. This single sentence made me feel physically sick. I have used that sentence before, probably more than once. So I know that it comes from the best possible place and with the best intentions. However, it still landed into the pit of my stomach, burning as if it had poisoned the lining.

"I'm sorry for your loss."

Even now it makes me feel sick; it's the word *loss* that lands the hardest. To lose something insinuates you have misplaced it, put something down and then forgot where it was. A bunch of keys, a mobile phone or some small change, objects that can be replaced. So why was it used in reference to my mother dying?

I hadn't misplaced her and she wasn't lost.

I hadn't lost hold of her hand in a supermarket and became separated. I couldn't put a poster up in hopes she came back. I never had a loss, it was much worse. Losing something means you have the hope of it returning but I didn't. My mother wasn't lost and she wasn't coming back, she was dead. My mother was gone and she would never be able to come back.

Events which alter your normality make you become aware of the smallest things. You really *hear* someone's words, *see* somebody's facial expressions and *interpret* someone's body language. Things that wouldn't normally have an impact on you stand out like a fireworks display. The first thing you notice is the glint of sympathy in people's eyes. All you can seem to now focus on is their uncomfortable and awkward twitching. Everything is heightened because you are emotionally exposed to everything.

You can't help but see and feel things differently to how you normally would. I felt anger towards things that I would have normally ignored and I felt sad towards things that would have normally made me smile.

If you're going through this right now just know what you are feeling is completely normal. It's totally ok and you are allowed to feel differently to how you once did (I wish someone would have told me this at the time.) I felt a lot of anger at the time and it confused me because naturally I am not an angry person. I understand now that it's ok to feel different, and to be different, because when you are completely exposed there are no rules. There are no rights and there are certainly no wrongs. My advice is, to go with every emotion you are feeling without trying to understand them.

Anyway I digress…after saying another goodbye to the nurses we turned back around and left. The next part of our hospital visit was to collect mum's medical certificate. I was silently struggling with this part of the day. I had already endured the worst but this was a different type of pain. Having to pick up a certificate that outlined mum's time, place and cause of death really meant it was final. Everything she had experienced in her life, all of the things she had accomplished, her personality and her legacy wouldn't be included. Instead she was summed up by what ended her life.

When we had the certificate we headed back home and I was emotionally drained. I had spent the whole day dealing with my emotions inside my head and it exhausted me. I was broken and falling apart inside. I had spent the day mentally sobbing my heart out but pretended I was holding it together.

The medical certificate displays the cause of death in the proper and medical terminology. Therefore, us mere mortals have a hard time trying to understand it. I'll show you how it was written and let you be the judge.

Cause of death:

I (a) Peritoneal and Lymphangiosis Carcinomatosis (b) Lymphoma

II Chronic Obstructive Pulmonary Disease.

After doing five different Google searches, all I understood was mum had cancer. It had spread and was already at the advanced stage. The cancer was within the cavity that surrounds the stomach, intestines, liver and other organs.

So despite her kicking its arse before it come back for vengeance. I guess mum won the battle but unfortunately cancer won the war.

Chapter Thirteen – Death Register

You are trapped inside a whole host of emotions when planning a funeral. You're at the starting line of the grieving process and there is an uphill battle to tackle. Yet before you can start that journey you have to plan the funeral. You have no control over what emotion hits you next or the regularity of them either. It hits you on an hourly, sometimes minutely basis. However you have to stay emotionally grounded during the funeral process because of the decisions you need to make. It's a battle between the two sides of the human brain, the emotional and logical side.

It feels abnormal planning the final goodbye for a person who, you can't imagine a future without. Your whole existence breaks into smithereens but you need to logically be finalising details. Now that we had the medical certificate we could finally register her death (yet another certificate needed.)

I just want to put it out there that I really hate the word certificate. Instinctively I associate it with success, accomplishments, rewards and celebrations. Definitions that shouldn't be used to describe the piece of paper that outlined my mother had died. This is proof that the most simplistic things become magnified. The days after mum had died rolled into a constant stream of hours. I couldn't tell you what day I did what on or what time I did what on. All I can remember was picking up the medical certificate and planning the funeral had happened within the same week.

I would logically guess that the funeral planning was on a Wednesday. On the basis I had been sleeping through the night since Sunday 10th January. It had only been three days since then and unbeknown to those around me, I was using the Codeine to help me sleep.

Looking back now I know that this was a disturbing and dangerous aid I had decided to lean on. I believed that without it I wouldn't sleep and I didn't want be drowning in my thoughts anymore. The Codeine allowed me to sleep and be lost in complete nothingness. I became dependant on the tablets quickly. I would never recommend or condone this method for the record. I am not ashamed or regretful though, I don't believe in having regrets. However I would not repeat or advise anyone using this as a coping mechanism.

Like all vices they weren't helping and all they did was mask things for a while. They gave me a hiding space from the things I couldn't face or want to deal with. The Codeine wasn't solving any of my problems at all. In fact if I had of continued down that road, I would have had a bigger problem right now. Vices give you an instant fix when you can't see any other way out, but when the effects wear off the problems resurface. What I failed to see was my problems weren't being fixed, and all I was doing was ignoring them. The longer I had ignored them and relied on tablets to make me sleep, I would have been a victim to their depths and I would have eventually surrendered.

In the grips of grief I could have easily become addicted to a very strong painkiller. It's the easiest thing to hide from your problems, but it doesn't mean it's the right thing to do. Behind the temporary fix of self-medication, everything you're hiding from is still there. You are simply prolonging having to deal with the problem by creating another.

Thankfully mine didn't become serious, and it only lasted two weeks (still two weeks too long.) My dad saw the Codeine in the medicine cupboard one afternoon. I kept it in plain sight because I didn't see it as an issue. I never looked at it as a vice, despite it being a part of my bedtime routine but I never saw it as a problem. However when my dad saw how many tablets had been taken, he threw them away. He knew about the one I took on Sunday because I told him and when he found the rest I was honest. I admitted to taking them to help me sleep and it was within that moment: the realisation had slapped me around the face. I heard the words aloud and hearing myself saying it I knew it wasn't ok.

My sleep did become a problem again after I stopped taking them. I was lucky if I got more than four or five hours a night. My problem was never solved by Codeine, it was just masked. It was still there and my mind reminded me my mother had died every single night. I couldn't solve this with a quick fix; I had a journey to embark on and it's one that I still battle with today. The moral of that short story is: don't hide behind a mask to fix a problem. Just because you don't see something it doesn't mean it's not there. As hard and as painful a situation might be you have to find the courage, and strength to fight back. Accept it and work through it, don't hide from it. You can only run so far until what you're running from catches you up.

Now back to the registration of mum's death and the funeral planning. Dad and I had decided to walk to the registry office. In fairness it was a twenty minute walk, but for anyone who knows me: knows I hate walking. I would get a taxi to my bed if I could. However I was grateful for the walk, I needed fresh air in my lungs and I wanted to distract my pacing brain.

When we got to the registry office we were told to take a seat and wait to be called in. The office itself was a newly built, one level hub and it reminded me a lot of a shed. All of the walls were clinical white and the smell of fresh paint was a little overwhelming (it reminded me of the reason we were there.) There were three rows of chairs that lined each side of the room, a reception desk and unlimited posters plastered everywhere. I remember the temperature of the waiting room was absolutely freeing too. It was the type of chill that instantly makes your jaw clench.

The beautifully sadistic thing about a registry office is that: you can have two families in the exact same room, but for completely different purposes. While we sat in the waiting room, a woman carrying a baby in a car seat and a man of similar age came in. Despite looking like they had lost any sense of what sleep was, they both had that glow of pride, happiness and completeness about them. They were here to register the birth, of what was quite clear to see, their bundle of joy. Directly opposite them sat me and dad. That wasn't the only thing we were opposites with, we were opposite in life too. They were there to record the start of a new life and, we were there mourning and recording the end of one.

I remember when I was younger being told that when one life ends, a brand new one starts. When someone dies a new life is born to replace that space in the world. On this day that description came to life, because here I was: a child registering the death of their parent, sat opposite a parent registering the birth of their child. I can't say that it made it any better or less painful but looking back on that moment; what I was told when I was younger is the way I think death should be told…a new soul is born into the world when another has left.

"Mr Price?"

Simultaneously me and dad had stood up and sucked in a small breath. Neither of us knew what to expect but, we were both anticipating a wretch of emotions. Dad took the lead towards the lady awaiting us and I followed behind refusing to take my eyes from the floor. When we had reached the room, it was another clinically white space. It was much more intimate and closed in, it was almost suffocating. The space was occupied by an overly large desk with a chair behind. There were two additional chairs in front of the desk, showing a clear seating arrangement. It felt very similar to an interview or how I would imagine an interrogation (ok maybe a little less intimidating that an interrogation, that was dramatic.)

The registration process started off incredibly formal with a handshake. I don't know why that particular moment has stuck in my memory but it has. I mean, it's a very normal greeting, but due to how emotionally charged I was at the time, the formal aspect of a handshake really stood out. We were given a prompt apology for our loss (by now was a normal conversation filler and it no longer meant anything to me.)

One thing I didn't expect though was all of the questions. I thought registering a death would be simple: hand over the medical certificate, confirm the details such as: address, age, marital status and place of death, but how wrong was I? We were bombarded with questions from mum's employment history to who her parents were. I think the only things we didn't get asked was: her favourite colour, pets name and her opinion on global warming. *How big was this death certificate going to be?* I mean with all the questions we were asked, I was picturing a hardback book to be published.

Dad answered most of the questions; in fact I wasn't much help at all. I just sat next to him desperately trying to settle my fidgeting hands and jerking leg (I was support for him in a really loose sense of the word.) His strength and courage was needed and it's something I can never thank him enough for. Here was this broken man, mourning the death of the person he loved like no other, answering questions as if he was filling out a questionnaire. She was the woman who gave birth to his child, the woman he shared over twenty years of life with, the woman he created memories with and the woman he cared for mentally, physically and emotionally. How he held it together is still a myth to me, he's always been and always will be my light, my hope and my strength.

After dad answered all the questions he needed to, we had to wait for the certificates to be printed. "How many certificates do you require?" *Surely we only needed the one right?* Wrong...another thing I never knew was every single company, associate and seemingly the whole world and his wife, needed a death certificate. The certificate they require must not be a copy either. Like any other human being, mum was involved with many companies, so dad requested ten certificates. There is a cost for the certificates too, £5.00 for each one (*you have to be kidding me* was my first thought.) This was another aspect I had no clue about, I didn't realise the registration of a death would cost a penny and still to this very day, this really annoys me (in fact it infuriates me.) A piece of paper that I don't want, but need by law is costing us money. *Isn't the fact I need the piece of paper certifying the death of my mother payment enough? Why should people be charged for a document that is a legal requirement?* I think it's despicable and disgusting that grieving loved ones are charged for a certificate of their grief.

It wasn't a choice, it wasn't a decision that we made and we never wanted to be registering my mother's death in the first place. This wasn't a booking, we weren't there to book a reservation or buy something. Me and my grieving father were there as a requirement by law to register the death of my mother. What's even more infuriating is without these documents, she couldn't be laid to rest. *How cruel is that?* It cost us £50.00 to have the ability to lay her body to rest. This is after she's already spent, sixty three years, working and having a percentage ripped out to pay the tax man.

Thankfully dad was aware of the protocol and he knew about the required payment so he didn't flinch. I would have loved to have seen my reaction, I can only imagine it being a picture. Anyway we now had the death certificates and could begin the process of laying mum to rest. Death truly is an eye-opening experience. It's not just the grief process or the heart breaking pain your body experiences. It's the small things which at the time have no apparent effect on you. Yet on reflection they have a significant impact on your outlook on life.

It seemed insignificant back then but I have a different perspective about death certificates now. I don't know how it works in other parts of the world but in the UK, this is a standard requirement for any death. This certificate doesn't contain anybody's social status, it doesn't state the memories the person created, it doesn't list any of that persons attributes, successes, failures, experiences or achievements. It doesn't state whether the person is good or bad, and there is no box to tick for heaven or hell. It literally states their profession, marital status and the cause of death.

Regardless what we achieve or what we don't or what we have or don't have, will never matter. We spend far too much time; in fact we waste too much time, focusing and stressing about bullshit. In the end it really doesn't matter, we all end up the same: listed on a register, a number in a database with the 'paid in full' checked off. We have an incredibly short space from birth to death, that time shouldn't be wasted worrying about conforming or ensuring we're acting in a certain way. We need to be living: however that may look to you, just live. Live the way you want and live the way you feel is right for you, as long as you're happy.

I didn't want this to sound like the typical: *'life's too short'* spill but, no matter how you change the wording, the meaning is still the same. We neglect the simplicity of just living and we all focus too much on things that in the end, doesn't matter. When I look at my mum's death certificate, all I see is formality, regulation and necessity. What I don't see is the conversations we had, the laughter we shared, the arguments we aired, her face, her touch, her voice and her stories. I see a piece of paper confirming a death, not a life.

I have to live a life time without her and I am unable to create new memories. It's only now I wish I could have had more time to make more memories. I don't wish that feeling on anybody so enjoy what you have. Make the most of the time you have, share it with the right people, and love it for all the right and wrong reasons. Don't end up being just a number, be more than that. Don't just exist make sure you live.

Chapter Fourteen – I Now Believe In Fate

Mum's death was now officially registered, all we had to do was make the funeral arrangements. The appointment with the funeral home was scheduled straight after the registration, so we made our way there. I was in complete numbing pain after registering the death; it was a different pain to what I had already experienced. Her passing did hurt beyond belief and I suffered unbelievable heartbreak but this just felt different.

Life was moving so fast around me but for me, my life was paused. It's a complex feeling to try and explain but I wasn't mentally or emotionally present in anything. All I wanted to do was make life pause and wait for me to catch up and to give me the chance to be present again.

Although we were arranging all the necessary things, mentally I was still sat on the floor at work, trying to process the news of being told my mother had died. I was completely absent to where I was and what I was doing. My body was moving into time zones that my mind hadn't yet recognised. Everything was happening too quickly and I wanted to stand still and scream. I felt suffocated and smothered by everything that was happening, and before I knew it, I was at another desk, opposite another lady, wanting to know the ins and outs of a ducks arse.

The funeral home we decided to use was *T Allen* funeral services. I had never been in a funeral home before so I didn't know what to expect. I honestly had no idea what I was doing, I mean what was there to expect from a funeral home? I don't know if I am the only one, but I had an eerie sense of peace and calmness. I had the persistent urge to whisper and I have no idea why, it's not like the dead can hear.

The lady (whose name for the life of me has vanished from my memories,) made you feel naturally at ease. I guess it's a part of her job making people feel relaxed in a time of desperate sadness. Dad did most of the talking again, I had the occasional input but for the majority it was all on dad. I really have no idea how he handled the whole day with the so much composure. I can never thank him enough for being so strong when he probably felt the weakest.

Planning a funeral for someone you love requires a level of emotional strength, which given the circumstances you don't have a lot of. The person you're planning the final goodbye for, is the only person you want to say hello to again. Like every step of the grieving process, you manage to make it through and before you know it…you're talking about different types of coffins.

It feels like your head and heart have been put through a blender, especially when you're flicking through a coffin catalogue. Morbidly different to the one memory of catalogue flicking I have. As a kid I was always given the *Argos* catalogue to circle the things I wanted for Christmas. Now here I was scanning over different styles of coffins for my mother's final place of rest. After we had a look through the world's most sinister catalogue, we were asked to decide whether it would be a burial or a cremation. Thankfully mum had already told us she wanted to be cremated, so that was the first decision made.

Although I respect my mother's final wishes (it is her body and she should decide how it's laid eternally.) I however secretly wanted a burial for mum, for no other reason but a selfish one. I wanted to have somewhere to go and talk to her and somewhere to be close to her again.

"Would you prefer to have a religious service or a life celebration?" was the next question. Despite having Catholic roots mum was not religious (she was probably more an atheist as I am,) therefore we decided to have a life celebration. We had made two of the biggest decisions, we had decided the type of service and how it would be delivered. The next question was whether we had chosen songs. For some reason this question made my stomach turn, it was as if it had caught my falling heart and was struggling to handle its broken shards.

I have always loved music, it's where I escape to and where I go to get voluntarily lost. I need to listen to music each day, it's the first thing I do when I wake up. When I need to concentrate I'll put music on, when I'm having a bath I'll have music on. Unfortunately I was never born with a musical gift, but it is still a big part of my life. As a child I would wake up on a Sunday morning, to the music of Sam Cooke, UB40, all the way to Tammy Wynette and Dolly Parton. For me music is one of the most powerful art forms and communication tools this world has. The way a song can connect with someone and can surface so many memories and emotions is astonishing.

When we were asked if we had chosen the music to be played at my mother's funeral, it caught me completely off guard. The answer was no, we hadn't spoken about songs at all and we hadn't heard music for days. I didn't know what time of the day it was, let alone what songs I want taunting me for the rest of my life. The songs we decide on will have a lifelong meaning to everyone who attends. These songs will forever be connected to her funeral each time they're heard. *How could I pick a song that summed up how I felt? I don't think there is a song that destroys you the second you hear it?* After sharing glances of dread, dad and I had both clearly neglected this aspect of the arrangements. Almost in a panic thinking we needed to decide then and there, we said we had no songs chosen. However we were quickly calmed and told we can get back to them, when we had the songs.

The arrangements were all finalised and we had decided on everything we could. All that was left was to set the date for the funeral and this was out of our control. The date and time was determined by the availability of the cremation chapel and life celebrants. Scanning through the vacant dates, the lady told us the earliest date that was available.

"Date: 1st February 2016

Time: 1:15pm

Place: Bluebell Hill crematorium."

Another fantastic start to yet another month of the New Year. We weren't even half way into January yet and 2016 is officially the worst year of my life. Eight days into the New Year, everyone was devoting time and energy to their New Year resolutions, but my family and I were trying to regain our balance after our world was obliterated. Not exactly the plans I had for the New Year. I had to endure an adjustment to my normality and I was about to experience a load of 'first times.' Let it be known that when someone tells you: "the firsts are the hardest to handle," they aren't lying. They are missing some fundamental information though... *all* the anniversaries and occasions are heart wrenching. It really doesn't matter if it's the first year, the tenth year or the fiftieth; they all hurt equally as much.

Life didn't seem to want to give me a breather. I'm certainly not the only person this has happened to and I won't be the last, but in the grips of darkness all you can think about is yourself. You find yourself in a shallow pool of self-pity and you can't understand why it's happened to you. You feel like you are the only one to have ever experienced it. Whilst I tried to understand how I would live now that my mother was no longer around, I failed to realise how many '*firsts*' were approaching.

After the funeral on the 1st February 2016 I endured Mother's day in March, Dad's birthday on the 16th August, Mum's birthday on the 30th August, my birthday on the 20th December, oh yeah, and…Christmas. It was our first Christmas without her (what a great thing to look forward to!)

Now that we had the date, time and location of my mum's funeral I felt overwhelmed. I didn't know what to do, say or think. *This was actually happening*; the reality of my nightmare was an incredibly hard pill to swallow. I knew that planning the funeral would be tough but when you hear the finalised details, it becomes more than words it becomes physical. Everything we had discussed and had decided will materialise and they will no longer be just words. I wanted to sink into the emotional ocean I was bottling up inside but I couldn't let go. Controlling my emotions had become a sadistic reward because they were something I could control. I had lost grip on everything else in life, but with my emotions I had the power of losing or keeping them. It was completely up to me.

Our meeting at the funeral directors was now complete (ironically my life had never felt so incomplete.) My life was falling apart, all around me and I didn't have an ounce of control over it. Dad and I shared our gratitude and goodbyes and left with heavy hearts and minds. We both wanted to fall onto our knees and detonate our heartbreak into the world. Instead we walked in silence, both choking back the lumps of pain that nestled in our throats. I know we both felt exactly the same as we both wore our pain and sadness on our faces. Our eyes were deep inside their sockets and both of our mouths shook in the corners. I had to constantly bite the inside of my cheeks, desperately trying not to cry.

I didn't want to be walking anymore and I just wanted to be at home. I didn't want to look at or even interact with another human being. As the silence grew louder and more suffocating, I broke it and just asked: "Can we get a taxi home?" Thankfully dad agreed and we walked to get one. The silence had now been invaded and we began idle talk. I took this as an opportunity and asked dad if he had any songs in mind.

He told me that there was a song which mum loved and that he thought about straight away. The only problem was he couldn't remember the title or who sang it, he said he would know it once he heard it but that was it. I could see in his face he was trying so hard to recall what the song was called. At the same time the sadness that his face wore, made me stop pressing on the subject. We had now walked for a good fifteen minutes and we were sat on a wall outside a medical centre, so we stopped and called a taxi from there. Once again we found ourselves in deafening silence but surprisingly, it was never awkward or uncomfortable. We both understood why and I think we were both too busy having a conversation with ourselves in our own heads.

The taxi arrived and being the gentle giant he is, dad opened the door for me before getting in himself. After telling the driver our address, he turned his head slightly towards me and whispered "This is the song." Playing on the radio was DJ Sammy – Heaven. The rest of the journey home was peaceful and the only sound was the radio. I wasn't someone who believed in signs or in fate. I was the annoying pessimistic Polly, who put things down to coincidences. Everything had to have a logical explanation because things don't just happen for any reason, but that all changed on that day. Maybe it was because I now had a reason to look for signs; I now had a person I wanted signs from. However to get a random taxi and the song that was playing, was the exact song my dad couldn't remember had to be more than just coincidence.

Even to this day I get shivers all over my body when I think about that taxi journey. The song wasn't in the charts and in fact it was released fourteen years previous to this moment. I remember I felt a strange sense of happiness; it was as if someone had given my pain a cuddle. I believe that my mother was in that taxi with us that day, and the song was her way of letting us know she was ok. I just felt too much security in that moment for that not to be true.

The hazy clouds of scrabbled memories are too far and in between for clarity. Some details are missing and after the taxi journey, my memory goes blank up until when I was lying in bed in the evening. I couldn't sleep so I tried to find songs for the funeral service. It was a welcomed distraction and gave me a purpose during my insomnia. It was however emotional torment I was inflicting on myself. I was searching for the saddest songs I knew and repeated them over and over.

Some of the songs made me cry but none of them reached me on a deeper level. I cried because they are sad songs and at the time I was the definition of sadness. These songs I would have cried to prior to my mother dying. I had basically listened to Adele's greatest hits, an Amy Winehouse cover of one of mum's favourite songs and still, nothing. I purposely avoided anything cliché: not the one from LeAnn Rimes, no Celine Dion and definitely no Whitney. I decided to look at songs by mum's favourite band and singer (for the record, I take no responsibility for my mother's taste in music.) Her music taste varied from gospel music, to country and then it would take a drastic redirection to G4 (if you even know who G4 are I am impressed, if you don't Google is your friend.)

Her favourite singer though was Gene Pitney and her favourite band was Westflife. I knew some of her favourite songs from them both as I heard them on more than the odd occasion. However I still wasn't getting that punch in the stomach like I thought I would. *Maybe I missed it? Maybe I'm too sad to feel that gut punch?* I continued to search for songs and then I found a Westlife song on YouTube. As soon as I heard the bridge and chorus, I knew instantly that it was the one (*as I sit here writing this part of the book, I put it on and I still get the same punch to my stomach and heart as when I first heard it.*) It summed up exactly how I felt, and it made me more than emotional, it totally broke my heart.

The signs never stopped appearing after the DJ Sammy song incident. I challenge anybody to try and prove me wrong on this - if you search for the Westlife song: *Close your eyes* on Apple music or Spotify the song will not come up. The song is on their Coast to Coast album but it doesn't appear on the streaming services and the only way I could play the song was through YouTube. This was another sign for me and therefore this had to be played at her funeral. I have added the lyrics and reading them in the present day I can relate even deeper than back then. *"You just close your eyes and you'll be here with me. Just look to your heart, and that's where I'll be. If you just close your eyes, 'til you're drifting away, you'll never be too far from me. If you close your eyes"*

We now had two songs for the service and had only one more to go.
I still needed to check with everyone if they were happy, or if they
wanted to change any. The third and final song I chose was a Gene
Pitney song (of course.) Mum was infatuated with him so it was only
right that one of his songs was played. It was just a case of getting
the right song and after searching for an hour, I found the perfect
song. I felt the punch in my stomach and my heart again. Without a
shadow of doubt this song made my heart crumble the most. The
lyrics are perfect and I believed every word, it said everything we all
wanted to say. *"When you say it's the end, I'll hand you a line and
I'll smile and say: don't you worry I'm fine, but you'll never know
darling, after you kiss me goodbye, how I'll break down and cry."*
I finally had all three songs selected, so I sent a link to all of the
songs to: my sister and brother to see if they were happy. I was given
the green light and that they agreed these were the perfect songs.
Mum's life was now going to be celebrated with a soundtrack. We
will all remember these songs for the rest of our lives and we won't
be able to listen to them again without thinking of mum.

Chapter Fifteen – Memory Lane

It had been a couple of weeks since mum had passed and life had got tougher and tougher. I was really struggling internally with my grief and my mind had become a harvest for dark and disturbing thoughts. My heart had become a dead muscle, it was cold and empty. I had no interest in anything anymore and nothing sparked any excitement within me. Any feelings that included happiness were also distance from me. I don't think I would have recognised the feeling if it had of slapped me.

I hated having any interactions with anybody and all I wanted to do was wallow at home in self-pity. Everything was too much effort, and mundane things needed energy, which I didn't have. I wanted to be in solitary, alone with my feelings and thoughts. No one understood how I felt or understood the thoughts I had. Having the feelings I had wasn't the worst part; it was the fact I didn't care that I had them, that was dangerous. I had lost all aspects of my nature, all the aspects of who I once was, but I didn't care about it. I tried my best to pretend I was ok but I wasn't fooling anybody but myself. More than anything I wanted people to believe that I was ok, because I wanted them to stop asking how I was feeling or how I was doing. I had a constant battle with wanting to scream about what was going on in my head, with just wanting people to leave me alone. It was much easier to say I was fine even when it was clear I was lying.

To me, I believed nobody understood how I was feeling. It wasn't because they didn't want to understand but physically, emotionally and mentally no one could. *All of these emotions, feelings and thoughts were inside of my body and my mind, so how could anyone understand that?* It was easier to say I was coping and doing ok instead of telling people the truth. It would have been too hard for people to hear that, I was drowning and loosing grips on my life. Nobody really wants to hear how much you're struggling because then they become obliged to help and advise you. Nobody knows what to say or do and there is no right or wrong (except anything you say or any advice you offer always feels wrong.) Grief is the result of losing a loved one and it traps a person's mind, body and spirit in a relay race of trauma. There will never be the 'right' thing to say or do which can change how a grieving person thinks or feels. It's like trying to tape back together a broken mirror. It might seem like the right thing to do, but the cracks are still there and it will never be the same again.

The truth is people don't understand how you feel within yourself, but some are able to understand the process you're being pulled through. Despite it feeling like you're the only human being who has experienced the death of a loved one, the obvious fact is you're not. There have been millions before you and there will be millions after you. More importantly, there are those around you and closest to you, who are also experiencing the grief at the same time. You feel like you're standing alone but when the mask of grief slowly peels away, you begin to notice the circle around you. If the *me* today had the opportunity to speak to myself back then, I would push myself to speak up earlier and lean on the support I had. I would tell myself to be brave and to stop hiding behind the pretence of being *fine*. At the time it's easy to feel annoyed, smothered and alone but believe me, when people are asking if you're ok, they really do want to know if you're OK.

I view grief as a germ because it spreads through every aspect of your being and your life. It slowly eats away at the person you was before and slowly changes the person you are. Like many germs when they fester long enough, they can create illnesses and conditions and although grief takes everything it can, it leaves you with much more than it takes. Everyone handles and is affected by grief completely differently. That's the twisted reality of grief, it doesn't discriminate. It doesn't have an instruction manual of how it will happen and what to do to overcome it and it certainly has no order or structure to its plans.

I soon found myself on a downward spiral to anxiety and depression. I never had these feelings and twisted thoughts before in my life. Nothing could have prepared me for the shark tank that is depression, but it was terrifying how quickly I accepted the feelings. I had stopped caring enough to want to change the way I felt, and I became comfortable with the deep sadness, anxiety and emptiness. I believed no matter what or how hard I tried, these feelings couldn't get better because my situation was never going to change. My mother had died and that was irreversible, this was my new normal and I had to adjust to the misery (the adjustment just happened too well and too quickly.)

Whilst all of these feelings had begun to invade my existence, mum's funeral was still pending. The meeting with the life celebrants was also still pending too. They needed to understand the woman we were all mourning. An appointment was scheduled for them to come and discuss mum at home, and the day was looming over all of us like a shadow of dread. Prior to all of this I had no idea what a life celebrant was but I knew that they would want to discuss memories. Having to reminisce who mum was and relay our memories terrified me. I wasn't ready to talk about her in any way, especially in a way that meant she was no longer here. I didn't want to do this, it wasn't fair and a part of me believed the more I ignored it all, it would go away. I was still deep in denial and continued to convince myself that she was actually still alive, and we would be told soon this was all a terrible mistake.

The ironic thing about grief is whilst you're feeling the deepest sadness you've ever felt; so enormous that even with imagination you couldn't understand it, there is still a part of you that genuinely believes it's all just a bad dream. Reality soon finds you and pummels you deeper into grief's awaiting embrace, it's a real life monster of manipulation.

It wasn't only in my consciousness where I hoped she was still alive. My brain had become that manipulated; my dreams and unconscious mind were tricking me too. I saw her face and all of her features, with no detail missing. I heard her voice and I watched her mannerisms. I could even touch her in every dream too. Suddenly I would be screaming her name and she would slowly fade away.

The worst dreams were the ones I was told she had died again; though these were never a replay of the actual day I was told. They were always new situations and they felt so real, I was forced to relive her death nearly every night. I felt like I had been thrown into the middle of the ocean during a storm, and every single time I tried to fight to stay above the water, the lower I sank and the weaker I got. Sometimes I will have days and moments I neglect the acceptance of her death. Days where I imagine her sitting on the sofa as I come home from work or demanding a hot water bottle because she's cold. It's not because I have forgot what happened because believe me that's impossible. It's purely my brain fantasising about my previous normality and wishing that it was still a reality.

The difference between having those fantasies today and having them so soon after she died is: I now accept and understand they're simply a fantasy and that it's not a possibility. Whereas before these brain malfunctions would tear off another piece of me and leave me even more exposed and broken. I was entering the gates of grief every day with fresh pain and it seemed like I would never leave. My emotions had locked me inside a cage and hid the key, I was trapped and I didn't have an escape plan. Each time mum was brought up in conversation, anxiety suffocated me. *I knew what had happened, everyone else knew what had happened, so why did we need to keep talking about?*

It was complete denial and I didn't want to accept she was gone. I preferred it when silence was the only surrounding I had. Silence gave me a place where reality didn't have to be faced and it was a place where my feelings didn't have to be discussed. However it was a double edged sword. I had found a space where I could avoid feeling anything and bask in my numbness, but it was a space that invited unlimited time to think. The silence and numbness didn't prevent my inner voice speaking to itself.

The day came where we had to talk about mum, about her life and about us. At this point my anxiety had grown fiercer and had become a lot harder to control. The idea of my broken hearted family members, having to talk and reminisce about mum in front of two strangers, made me feel sick to my core. It came far too quick for my liking but sat in my living room with me was my dad, mum's sister Patsy, mum's brother Steve, mum's brother Malcolm, my sister and my brother. The room was filled with uncertainty and it clung to the air like a cheap air freshener. None of us wanted to say anything in the fear we would say something wrong. All of us had so much to say but none of us had a way of saying it. It was a room of relatives who were hurting together. We were connected by pain and ancestry, yet it felt like a room full of strangers. The uncomfortable silence was broken by a knock at the door and I took the deepest inhale of air, and I held it until the pressure in my chest reminded me to exhale.

As the door opened two ladies walked in and found their positions on the sofa. Instantly, their presence lifted the room and the uncomfortable silence was broken. "Hey guys, I'm Nicky and this Debbie. We're the life celebrants from Memory Lane." The rapport was immediate and I knew instantly they was the perfect people to do mum's life celebration. I whole heartedly believe mum would have approved of them. As the time passed their personalities grew and just like my mother, they were not hung up on airs and graces (thankfully.) They simply got us as a family and we all just clicked, I felt like I had known them for years.

Whilst everyone shared stories Nicky and Debbie made notes in their notebooks. They managed to do this without losing any eye contact or our engagement. In reflection we were all submerged in remembering mum so we didn't pay too much attention to what anyone else was doing. There was one observation I wasn't oblivious to because it made me feel exposed and confused. Every so often I was drawn out of the room and the conversation by the feeling of being watched. It's a sixth sense feeling that someone is watching you. It's unsettling because you can never normally locate the eyes that are on you. The feeling I had was the same, many of you can relate to, but the difference was I located the eyes that were watching me. As I followed the direction I felt the stare, I was met with the eyes of Nicky. This wasn't a trickery of the mind and my feeling of being watched wasn't just a feeling. I was being watched but I didn't know why? The conversation was happening around me and I was simply there listening. *I had not said anything so why was I so visually important?*

When I caught Nicky's gaze she smiled and looked back to the direction of the conversation. It wasn't the typical rush of panic that you have when someone catches you staring. It was slow and unapologetic. *Maybe I had let out a noise? Maybe I did actually say something? Maybe I am officially going mad?*

I timidly smiled back trying to disguise my uncomfortable confusion. The conversation began to flow once again and dad began telling the story of how he and mum met. I was smiling throughout just like everyone else because it's a funny anecdote. However I was once again distracted by that same sixth sense feeling of being watched. This time I didn't hesitate, I knew where the eyes were located so I snapped my attention back to Nicky. She briefly focused on dad and the conversation, but before I could look away, Nicky's head swung back to me. It was as if I had called her name and she held her gaze for longer than I felt comfortable with. Her face looked happy like she was glad to see me, which is totally weird considering we don't know each other.

Her eyes were connected with my face for what felt like hours. I shuffled around to try and shake off her fixation but it failed. Part of me wanted to ask what her problem was and why she kept staring at me, but then I really saw the stare. I realised that she wasn't staring at me she was staring right through me. I know how that sounds but I felt the urge to look behind me. She had zoned out of her conscious and then her eyes flicked to my face accompanied with the same smile as before. Then she diverted back to the room and the conversation as if nothing had happened. I now really felt uncomfortable and I did not like that at all. I wanted to move and sit somewhere else, preferably where she couldn't physically see me. That wasn't an option so I ignored the other sixth sense feelings I felt, and continued with the conversations and offered the occasional input.

Once we had finished sharing stories and memories about mum, Nicky and Debbie shared their history and who they were. Knowing more about them and what they've done professionally, helped confirm that they were the right option. They were both so down to earth and their sense of humour was in line with all of ours. There was one thing that they shared which made the hairs on the back of my neck stand on end. Aside from being life celebrants, they were both mediums. Although I was brought up by a mother who was a fan of mediums, I was not. For me (as a very sceptical being) the act of being able to communicate to the dead was a violation and manipulation of a person's vulnerability. A profession built on the skill of knowing how to feed on someone's emotions. To me it was a profession that exploited the desperate desire to reconnect with a loved one.

Mum used to make me watch TV shows with her about mediums. There would be a whole room of people, hoping for a stranger to reconnect them with the non-living. I always criticised the shows because of course at least one person in that room will be able to relate. The medium would inform the room that they "have a gentleman trying to come through, holding his chest." Now in a room of say, fifty people the probability of someone in the room having lost a loved one to a heart attack would be high. Yet despite having scepticism for mediums, when I heard that the women who were planning my mother's funeral service, were also mediums it made me shiver.

I don't know why it had an impact on me, on my physical feelings and especially my mind. Maybe it was a 'in that moment' thing? My emotions were high and the denial that my mum had died played a huge role in the weird feeling I had. *Was I hoping that they would tell me mum was here? Was I hoping they had a message from her?* I don't know but I couldn't shake it from my thoughts and it had freaked me out.

We wrapped up the afternoon and truthfully it wasn't as bad as I had pre-empted. None of us cried, I anticipated flood gates galore but thankfully it didn't happen. I think it was the first time we had all genuinely smiled and laughed and not just for pretend. The gut wrenching sadness you get after laughing and smiling at a memory is excruciating. You're hit with the realisation that memories are all you have left and it will be impossible to create more. Someone you love unconditionally will always have your heart burning and your mind full with memories. When they're no longer here the memories turn that burning feeling into a scorch and they drown your mind with its fullness.

You will never understand why it's important never to take any moment for granted, until you're faced with not being able to see a loved one again, and know that no more memories will be made. We never know when it's the last time we will see someone, but when it happens, all we have left are memories. We won't have the opportunity to make plans, to forward think into the future. Everything becomes about the past, about what we did or didn't do. Everything becomes a memory and we will never be able to build more with that person.

When that last day comes with your person, make sure when you're walking down memory lane, there's plenty of scenery. Don't allow your memory lane to be about all the things that you didn't get to do or didn't say. Your memory lane should be a place you never want to leave.

Chapter Sixteen – Please Be Upstanding For The Committal

1ST February 2016 was the second worst day of my life so far and equally the most stressful day I have ever experienced. Officially one month into the brand new year. Resolution commitments were either being honoured or broken. It was also twenty three days since my mother had passed away. Exactly twenty three days since my life fell into a dark, empty and painful existence.1ST February 2016 was when my mum's body would be laid to its eternal resting place. The service was scheduled for 1:15pm at Medway Crematorium.

It was the day I had to sit and watch the wooden box that held my mother's peaceful frame, be committed into the hungry burning flames. Watching your loved one be committed to their forever resting place is something we all know will eventually happen. Yet when that time comes it seems incredibly sinister and abnormal.

The night before was a rough battle between me and sleep and it was one I didn't win. Every minute of the night was filled with anxiety, heartbreak and paralyzing fear. I didn't know what I was scared of, maybe it was because it had become final. With the absence of sleep, it was soon morning and time for me to face the dreaded day.

The atmosphere around me was heavy and suffocating. The house was stonily silent and the feeling was overwhelming. I wished I didn't have to do this. I remember going into the bathroom for some space, but it didn't calm me down because I tried to plan the perfect way I could run away. I toyed with numerous excuses I could give as to why I needed to pop out and never come back. This made my anxiety worse. I now felt sick, scared and under increased pressure for some reason. Instead of running I cemented my body on the sofa in the living room.

I knew the day would be painful in ways I wasn't ready for. I thought the most pain I'd ever experience in my life would be the day mum died, but here I was on the day of her funeral and the pain ripped my chest apart. I struggled to catch my breath, it didn't hurt any more or any less, it hurt differently. It was a new pain and another new reality my normality had to adjust to again.

As the morning moved into afternoon, the impending realisation of what was going to happen made my body heavier. My anxiety had reached a new high and it controlled every inch of my body. My mouth had lost all functionality and any desire to talk was muted. My hands were covered in sweat and had uncontrollably shook. My chest got tighter with every second that went past. In my head I was still trying to form a plan to leave and to run as far away as I could. People soon began walking in and out of our house and they started to line up outside. I heard so many voices all talking at the same time, they morphed into each other and became unbearable noise. I wanted them to shut up, leave and never come back. I was engulfed into numerous embraces but none sparked any feelings from me, it just felt as if the air was being thrown out of my body. This would be the day I watched my mother's coffin burn, so I couldn't and also didn't want to feel any affection either.

Mum's brothers arrived and went straight into the kitchen where dad was. He was trying to find a place to hide too, both of us didn't want to make small talk. We didn't want to hear how sorry for us people were. We both unconsciously avoided each another most of the morning too. We barely had enough strength for ourselves, let alone each other.

I heard muffled voices, broken sentences and whispered cries coming from the kitchen. I closed my eyes and released a solitary tear, immediately wiping away the evidence with the back of hand. Hearing my uncles and father comforting each other's heart break, only made my heart shatter further. I looked at the ceiling hoping that gravity would push the tears back down that were threatening to spill out. Then I heard the words I didn't want to know: "She's here."

This one sentence impaled my eardrums and left the echo ricocheting throughout my body. If only it had a different meaning, and she was actually here. The two words made my whole body want to shut down. My legs were instantly frozen and weighted down; my hands were drenched in sweat. I had the burning ache in my jaw telling me I was close to throwing up and my stomach felt hollow with bolts of electric shooting around inside. Whilst all of these physical feelings bullied my body, the one physical pain I felt more present than any other was the intolerable ache in my chest. It shot across my shoulders and arms and I thought I was having a heart attack (*great, how bloody ironic.*)

A little dramatic I know but thankfully I didn't have a heart attack. However my heart was being attacked and it was broken. I honestly didn't know how much more damage it could handle. The physical pain you feel from true heartbreak is worse than the initial sense of sadness. I had no idea how I would survive this day, I couldn't even think about getting up from the sofa. If I had a choice not to go I would have taken it quicker than a breath but I didn't have a choice. I had to go whether I wanted to or not and the acknowledgment of that, made me hurt more.

I have been to funerals prior but they were people who I wasn't closely attached to. I didn't have that bond with most of them that made pain run my existence. I felt the sadness (I'm not completely stone hearted) but I felt the sadness more from the energy of others. At a funeral where you're paying your respects, you're surrounded by the sadness of loved ones. When you're not closely associated with the person, you can separate your emotions. However, when you attend a funeral for a person you have a connection with emotionally and genetically, the sadness you experience is overwhelmingly different. It is entirely different to anything you've known or felt before.

You are no longer surrounded by other people's sadness, you're not feeling or feeding off other people's sadness. Instead, you're sunken by sadness, it's controlling your whole being and you're now the feeder of sadness for those around you.

I was owned by fear and was chained down by the anxiety racing through my body. People were now beginning to spill back out the front door and preparing for the drive to the service. Each time another person left the house, the pressure and realisation that I would soon be next and have to walk outside choked me. I knew I would be surrounded by an army of sympathetic and sad faces. I wouldn't only encounter them the once because they would be following behind us, on the way to the pending flames mum's body would be wrapped in.

How on earth am I going to be able to walk outside of my house? My legs didn't feel like they would be able to hold me up and my heart was walloping behind my ribcage. I managed to pull myself up from the sofa, and I found myself standing in front of the window. I tried to look past the tears that had built up inside my eyes and all I could see was the blur of the car.

I saw a shiny black stretched car sat in the middle of the road. The windows were so clean that they glistened in the daylight, but as the saying goes "all that glistens is not gold." The most tragic but beautiful image I had ever seen, laid behind all the glisten and shine. An image I wish I didn't have to see but it's a sight that I can never forget. Looking beyond the shine and glisten, I saw a lightly varnished wooden box. It was centred in the car's interior, and it was bordered with flowers. Resting inside this eternal wooden bed was the woman who had given me life. She had spent hers ensuring mine was the best it could have been and now I was about to close the final chapters of her. I wanted this to be a horrific dream but it wasn't and I wasn't going to wake up anytime soon. This was reality, it was my reality and I hated every second of it. In fact, I've had better nightmares.

It was time to face my reality, my newest fear and my real life invitation to hell. It was time to leave and my legs felt the increasing pressure to support my quivering body. I flashed my eyes to the ceiling and snatched the air around me. I needed a minute of composure so I could walk. I inhaled as deep as I could without passing out and when breathing became a problem, I released the air from my lungs and slowly opened my eyes. I didn't have time to catch up with my feet, they carried me outside and before I knew it I had an overbearing attachment of eyes on me. I dropped my head down and fixed my eyes on my feet. I didn't want to see peoples' faces, their pity, their sorrow and their sadness. I wasn't ready for that. The closer I got to the car, the more I felt people's breath on me. Everything was getting too close to me and I felt claustrophobic. My breathing quickened with each step and despite being outside I felt enclosed.

I was having a panic attack, it wasn't an obvious one and I wasn't hyperventilating. I didn't show a sign of panic on the surface but inside was a whole different story. I compare my anxiety and panic attacks with a duck. It glides across the water composed, yet under the surface its legs are frantically flapping. This is how I feel when I have an attack. I look fine on the outside but inside it's like a snow globe has been shaken in a blender.

Finally my hand reached door handle and I gripped it so hard that my knuckles turned white. It gave my legs some much needed support and stability. My head was still fixed to the ground below and I didn't engage with any eye contact. I needed to get in the car and quickly. When I opened the door I found the safety of the seat and closed the door. The air I had been holding onto fought its way out along with a sigh of relief.

I never realised how incredibly slow a funeral procession was until I was a part of one. As the car stalked the hearse, my heartbeat began to normalise and it became bearable to breathe again. I bowed my head and focused on my fidgeting hands. I've seen a funeral procession before and I know that you can see inside the cars, so I kept my head down because I couldn't bare anyone's pitiful eyes (especially strangers.)

The only time I looked up I was instantly hit with regret. As we approached a mini roundabout, the hearse went around the bend first and the side of the coffin caught my attention. I was unable to pull my gaze away until I saw the warmest smile I had seen in a long time, I was staring into my mum's eyes. I was fixed on the photograph of mum that had been placed at the foot of the coffin, I desperately longed for her expression to change. The panic I felt before came crashing back into my chest. I wanted to open the door and run away as fast as I could but I was shackled to the seat and still entranced by mum's face. I hadn't noticed the tears that had built up in my eyes, until I felt one escape. As the tear ran down my cheek, I closed my eyes and threw my head back on the head rest. Thankfully the procession had picked up in speed and we were no longer crawling along the roads. I managed to regain my composure and I made the conscious decision, not to look out of the window again.

The journey felt like it would never end but given the destination, this wouldn't have been the worst thing. I think we stopped at every red traffic light known to man, and the closer we got to the crematorium the faster my heart raced. Knowing I had to exit the car and physically be around all the people who had come to pay their respects, pushed the bile from my stomach up into my mouth. I felt increasingly panicky again and it felt like a wall was being built inside my body. It felt impossible to breathe or concentrate, I wanted the car to turn back around and take me away. I would have settled to drive miles and miles with no destination in mind. I wanted to be anywhere else other than in the middle of my reality.

As the car turned into the gates, my head felt exceptionally heavy and I couldn't lift it to look forward. My eyes stayed focused on the floor underneath my feet. My mind had vanished and I was back into the state of numbing emptiness. All I could concentrate on was the heaviness of my head as it started to gravitate lower and lower. I heard a choir of sighs, as each one of us in the car released the air trapped in our lungs. The first time since I had got into the car, I acknowledged the presence of others. The unified sighs signalled that we were closer than I wanted to be to the chapel, and closer to the start of the final goodbye I didn't want to have.

I lifted my head up and glanced out of the widow, I was instantly slapped with regret again. The car had parked in the middle of the driveway that housed the chapel at the end and freshly cut grass covered each side of the driveway. Despite all of my surroundings, my eyes couldn't be torn away from the number of figures surrounding the car. Everyone who was paying their respects wore sadness and pity on their faces, and each face was attached to the car: I felt the burn of their eyes. Their stares were all over my body and they pierced my skin leaving me even more exposed. My entire body froze on the spot and the panic I had managed to compose, began to tremble out. It was becoming progressively difficult to control my breathing. Each time I inhaled, the air felt as if it couldn't circulate around, so I rushed getting the exhale out and before I knew it I was hyperventilating. I remember repeating over and over that I needed to get out of the car. The air inside had become toxic and my chest was heaving.

My heartbeat raced just as fast as the seconds that went by and the panic grew stronger. I wasn't only panicking from not being able to breathe, but I feared each face I saw. They were getting closer and closer to the car and it felt like I was in a real life horror film. For whatever reason, in that moment I felt like I was going to die (obviously not by a killer but I felt like I was going to be crushed.) I was either going to be crushed by my own lungs, or I was going to be crushed by all the people surrounding the car.

I had never in my entire life felt more scared than I did waiting inside that car. I was drowning in panic and I was frozen in complete fear. I squeezed my eyes shut as hard as I could, I desperately wanted to block out every single feeling and thought I was having. Then I felt a cold breeze hit me around the face. The driver had opened the car door and my lungs grabbed every inch of the new air surrounding me. Without a second thought I swung my legs out and my body followed. I have never exited a car faster than I did that day, and as soon as my shoes found the ground, it felt like everyone took one hundred steps back. The reality of their distance had become clear and the illusion I was suffocated by had vanished. Their expressions of sadness and pity hadn't vanished though, and they made me feel sick.

I don't recognise any face in particular, I was just bombarded with a sea of familiarity and they all blurred into one. There were so many people, so many faces and too many bodies, it was overwhelming and too much to process. Though looking back, it's overwhelming for a different reason. Mum had so much love surrounding her that when she was alive, you'd take it for granted. All of these people had come to pay their respects to my mum, which meant she had impacted their life. My mum will forever have a lasting effect on my life, on my choices and has become my purpose. However, I had never released what she meant to others in her life.

The closer we got to the chapel the louder the sound of the first song became. I was pulled into embraces but I have no idea who these embraces were with. We stopped at the entrance and stood behind the open hearse. Nicky and Debbie stood at the open doors of the chapel and welcomed us with small smiles. Something about the way they smiled at you was completely different to the way others did. They never masked theirs with sympathy, it was always with warmth and it instantly gave me a sense of calmness.

"Would anybody like to carry the coffin?"

It absolutely will not be me…not going to happen. Although the offer was only open to my uncles, my dad, brother and nephew, I still said no in my own mind. However, there was a resounding choir of no's echoing back. The look of complete emptiness and pain on all of their faces, explained why they couldn't do it. Then out of the silence was a delicate and broken voice.

"I'll do it."

All of our heads followed the direction of the voice and standing with his head high, eyes visibly glazed with tears and a face with controlled sadness was Harry. He was her baby, her world and he was going to carry her down to her final spot. My heart broke had splintered, there wasn't much left to break anymore. He's little face didn't flinch, he stood so tall and so ready. This is the last clear memory from that day, everything else has vanished. The whole day was unreal and is now a blur. After sitting down for the first time in the chapel, I am unable to remember anything else from the service and it tears me apart. I can't remember the day we paid tribute to her and that destroys me daily.

All I have from that day is the start of the morning, sitting down in the chapel and then me rushing to the exit as soon as I heard: "please be upstanding for the committal." As soon as I heard those words, I couldn't watch the curtains draw to a close whilst her body was taken. I needed air, my lungs were tight and they felt as if they were evaporating in my throat. As I ran through the exit, fresh air smashed into my face and finally into my lungs. Every emotion flooded my body, my face was drenched in my tears and my mouth stung from the taste of bile.

Chapter Seventeen – I Want To Be Normal Again

The reality of mum's death, her absence from my world had started to rip into my life. I was broken and exposed with pain being the only consistency. Every day after mum had passed away the house was filled with visitors offering their condolences. I had something to distract my mind each day, and it gave me a break from the torture grief lined up for me. Although I felt the emptiness in my heart and the loneliness in my soul, I hadn't succumbed to its grip on me yet. This changed when mum's body was laid to rest. When she was cuddled by the flames of eternity, the visits became less and less and the true absence of her shadowed on each of our days. The empty space on the sofa where she used to sit became larger each day. Her coat hung up redundantly and it grew visible each second of each day. I was surrounded by everything of hers and all that she owned and I was enclosed in her world, yet her absence from it ran circles around me. Despite everything of hers being so close, I was reminded every day of how far away she was.

My mental health was becoming more unstable and my thoughts and feelings lingered in darkness and despair. I had never had problems with my mental stability, but I was left confused by the effects of bereavement. Obviously I knew that mental health existed and how other people struggled with it, but I couldn't relate to how rough it was, when I never struggled. I had heard about depression and I've known people who've experienced depressive states. However I had never personally experienced those levels of deep sadness and turmoil before. It was now happening to me and I had those feelings I've heard about. I related to people who couldn't and didn't want to get out of their beds in the morning. I could understand how they had no interest or excitement in anything. Nothing made me feel happy anymore and there was nothing I wanted to smile about: I felt miserable, broken and empty. My outlook on life was negative and dark and my thought process jumped from: *what is the point in anything, to, I don't care about anything or anyone.*

I was surrounded by all the support I could have needed but I still felt unbelievably alone. I was lonely and lost and what made matters worse was I wanted to be alone all the time too. I wanted to wallow in self-pity, and give in to my depression. The feeling of deep sadness and despair had become the only thing I felt close to and I saw depression as a comfort in a twisted way. I look back now and I see how it was the root of evil for how I felt and thought. I had neglected that people around me were also grieving, and I didn't accept that they felt the sadness of mum's death too. I believed I was struggling alone and that nobody understood what I was dealing with in my heart and mind.

I went back to work fairly soon after mum had died as well and it had both good and bad aspects. Having a slither of normality back in my life distracted my thoughts and feelings for most of the time. Work gave me something to focus on other than the gaping hole in my heart. However the distraction was a façade, I never stopped thinking and I certainly never stopped hurting. I couldn't focus as well as I needed to and I struggled finding a balance to my internal mayhem. My mind was in a complete shamble and I was making stupid mistakes. I became oblivious to details and I had also drawn short of patience. I was drowning and I could barely keep my head above water. I didn't want the pity party from anyone but it was hard to keep up the pretence of being *OK*. My temper had also found itself on its last thread, and the smallest things would make my blood boil. I was a coiled spring and it only took one wrong comment and I would unleash a wrath of venom, but this didn't just happen at work. My anger was affecting my whole life and I became unbearable to be around.

I would look at strangers, people who I had never laid eyes upon before and I would get this urge to hurt them. I felt an uncontrollable anger boiling inside of me for absolutely no reason whatsoever (they didn't need to do or say anything.) It's not in my nature to be violent and any kind of confrontation turns me into an anxious and uncomfortable mess. Yet I wanted to inflict pain on anyone that my mind took a disliking to. Thankfully I didn't follow up on any of the urges but this only made my anger even worse. I don't wish I had punched a stranger in the face, but I should have done something with the pent up anger. Instead I continuously swallowed all those feelings over and over again (should have just bought a punch bag!)

My personality had done a one eighty and the person I had become was a stark contrast to who I was before. I knew I had changed and I hated the person I was turning into but I played ignorant. I denied any acknowledgement of the changes and I would brush it off every time. My typical excuse would be "I'm just having a bad day," yet in reality I was actually having the worst time on a daily basis. There was no such thing as a *bad day*, because every day was either the same as the last one or I would feel lower than the one before. I didn't want to have fun anymore and I had lost all sense of meaning for that word. I didn't look forward to anything either, all I wanted was to stay at home doing nothing. I didn't want to think, talk or feel because everything and everyone (for no fault of their own,) annoyed the living hell out of me.

As timing would have it the year before mum died, I had booked a holiday to Las Vegas for April 2016 with my closest friends. We were all ecstatic and we couldn't wait to live life up in Vegas (hopefully not find ourselves in a chapel getting married to an Elvis impersonator.) Mum and dad gave me spending money as a Christmas present (quite a bit to be honest,) they were both excited for me. Mum was especially excited, Vegas would be right up her street if she wasn't such a big baby and could get herself on an aeroplane. She was a gambling maniac so she would have been in her element. Despite her having no intentions of leaving the UK, she was always excited to see the world through the pictures I had taken. So when I booked Vegas, I knew she would want to see everything the place had to offer.

It was four months after mum died and Las Vegas was approaching, it was going to be the holiday of a lifetime. My excitement was now tarnished with the pain in my heart, the loss in my soul and the hatred I had for life. If I could have I would have stayed home and missed the whole trip. I was no longer eager or excited to go anymore and the reality of being 5,253 miles away from home was making me feel sick. Regardless of how much I wanted to stay at home I did go. I boarded the flight and I spent a week in Las Vegas with the girls and I tried desperately hard to have a good time. Dad was the main reason I decided to go. He had persisted that I needed the break and reminded me how mum would have gone ballistic if I wasted all that money by not going (I hate it when parents are right!)

Ironically it was the best trip I have ever taken and it's the most incredible place in the world. It was an eye opening and life long memory I will keep forever. Yet despite being in the most incredible place on earth, it still didn't take an inch off the pain I felt. Each day I woke up, I was reminded how my life had changed. I couldn't block out any of my thoughts or my pain and my guilt wreaked havoc with my mind every minute. Each time I smiled, laughed or had a good time I was struck by guilt. *How can I have a good time, a happy time in Las Vegas when only months previous, I was at my own mother's funeral? Why do I deserve to enjoy myself? What is the point?* I had also left my dad alone while I lived life up in Vegas. *How can I be so selfish?* These were all the thoughts haunting my mind.

Whilst I masked the pain with a smile and pretended that I was fine, all I wanted to do was sob my heart out. It wasn't all torture though…I did have a good time and the guilt I felt was representative of that. Some days I was given a few hours free of depressive thoughts and for brief moments I had a taste of happiness again. It was a bitter sweet experience and I am grateful for the adventure and the memories. That trip was the epitome of being shown hope and the light at the end of a tunnel. It showed me that despite the ugliness of life, there was still beauty that needed to be explored. I realised that I still had a life and it needed to be lived. Hindsight is a wonderful thing because if someone would have told me that at the time, I probably would have punched them in the face (only joking…maybe.)

The hardest part of Vegas was returning home because I had convinced myself that I had no right to feel sad because I had been on holiday. I began to torture myself again with all possible scenarios. I role played what I thought people would have said if I was depressed about mum and I heard the disgust in their invisible voices. This is what happens when you believe the stigmas around mental health. When you believe that a person can't smile or possibly laugh if they're depressed and they certainly can't have, what someone else perceives as 'fun.' We're made to believe that if you have depression, you must be sad all the time and you must be in bed twenty four seven, crying into your pillow.

The reality is you can be smiling, laughing, happy, sad and crying into your pillow all at the same time, and that's why it's exhausting. It's also tiring when you have to defend your choices, your moods, your feelings and your behaviours to people; when they still choose to make their own assumptions, rather than trying to understand. In my experience with depression I never truly felt happy. I always felt sad but I hated feeling like that, so I tried to do things that cracked through the sadness. Did this mean that I was cured? That I was no longer in a depressive state? That because I had smiled for the first time in days, weeks and months, I was no longer depressed?

The answer is no…plain and simple.

Depression doesn't just go away and it isn't cured with a smile or a laugh. It can't be forced out of you and you certainly can't simply 'get over it." Depression is a mental illness and like any physical illness, it needs to be treated correctly. If you know someone going through depression be patient, be present and be available. The worst things you can be are frustrated, angry and distant with them. They are still the same person you knew before and they will always be that person. Depression is not everything a person is, it's only a part of who they currently are. Don't pressure them to get better, because that's all they want, but it's also everything they're scared of doing. They are scared in case it doesn't work and then they will lose any hope they may have had.

Putting pressure on someone to get help really makes them feel like a worthless piece of crap (I'm just throwing that out there.) They do want help and they don't want to feel the way they do, but they don't feel good enough or worthy of happiness. It's your tough job as the loved one, to show them that they *are* enough and they *are* worthy of happiness. Please do not guilt trip them either as it doesn't help. Making someone feel like they are affecting your happiness or life in a bad way, will make their depression grow into an engulfing fire around them.

You will find yourself frustrated, angry and helpless and you'll probably want to run as far away as possible, and that is ok, they're your emotions and feelings. However remember your loved one has emotions and feelings too, ones they don't want or understand but don't know how to stop. Unless you're a mental health professional you will always say or do the wrong things. You will never say the right things because you act on love and fear, so encourage help from specialists and support where you can. If you are fighting with your mental health, don't neglect the fact that you always have a choice. It will always be hard to reach out for help but it's not a sign of weakness and it's not you admitting to being crazy.

You'll be fine soon right? So what would be the point in wasting time? Having a mental illness is as serious as having a physical one. If you broke your arm you wouldn't ignore the pain and hope it goes away. If your bone had cut through the skin, you wouldn't throw a jumper over it so people would think you're ok. You would seek medical advice and fast because that's normal. So why is your mental health any different? Why is it any less important to go get help for?

It is no different and it certainly isn't any less important, just because you can't see it or other people can't see how unwell you are, doesn't mean you're OK. It doesn't matter how hard or how much you don't want to get help. Is suffering any easier? Would you prefer to have the thoughts and feelings you have, over not having them? There is honestly no logical reason or explanation as to why you shouldn't and cannot get help. Every reason and explanation you have for not getting help comes solely from fear. It's incredibly normal to feel nervous, scared and apprehensive about getting help, but it's scarier not being able to accept your worth and potential. Everybody in the world deserves to be happy but it cannot be given to you. Nobody can give you happiness because it's already inside of you and you're the one who is responsible of finding it, building it and nurturing it.

We will all at some point in our lifetimes feel and experience pain. Some will feel it on grander scale than others, some for a longer time than others, and maybe more painfully than others, but we will all experience pain nevertheless. That's life and how it works, we have no control over it. However we do have the control over if we suffer: we all have that choice. We choose if we will suffer and how long we will suffer for.

I lasted four months... it was four months after my world shattered underneath me and I was dropped into the open arms of depression, that I decided to reach out and get the help I needed. It was the most terrifying thing I've done and I had every second thought you could imagine when I sat in my doctor's surgery. I was crippled by anxiety and all I wanted to do was get up and walk out. My hands were sweating from every pore and my stomach was back flipping like an untrained gymnast. It would have been the easy option for me to give up and cave into the fear rippling through my body. I could have gone back home and pretended I was fine and I could have accepted this was it and lose myself to this illness.

That would have been the easiest thing to do, but I chose the other option. I swallowed the urge to vomit and pushed myself to stay. I didn't know what was happening to me and I didn't like it, all I wanted was to be normal again. Therefore I made the decision not to suffer anymore, I chose to get help.

<u>Chapter Eighteen – Happy Pills</u>

I grew up believing that anti-depressants never work, they simply made people dependant and it was near impossible to stop taking them. I would hear how 'so and so' had been on happy pills for years and how they should face up to things and get out the house. How they simply just had to get over it and that they didn't need the tablets. These small comments I had heard constantly in my childhood, affected how I viewed things as an adult.

I knew no different and I believed what I had heard around me. So when I booked a doctor's appointment to discuss my mental state I was terrified that they would prescribe me these happy pills that did nothing. As I sat in the waiting room and fought the urge to run out the door I heard a beep. I looked up to the electronic board and my name was there...I was next. I felt my fight or flight mode kick in but before I could choose a side, my autopilot had switched itself on. My feet had carried me across the waiting room and onto the chair in doctor's office. There I was opposite my doctor and the panic rushed through my body. I didn't even know what to say. *What do I need? Why am I seeking medical advice? Am I wasting everybody's time?*

"Miss Price, what can I help with today?" I know I needed to ask for help but I didn't know what to say. I was overwhelmed by emotions and I had to use everything I had to stop myself from breaking down. I knew that if I cried I would definitely be given them stupid tablets. I managed to keep it together and I was completely honest with how I was feeling. It was the first time I had told someone exactly how I was feeling, of course I left some details inside of my head (like wanting to punch strangers in the face.) I felt vulnerable and bare because I had finally admitted that I was struggling. I explained how I struggled to sleep and eat after mums passing. I admitted that every day I felt incomprehensible sadness and even the idea of going for a walk made me want to vomit.

Once I had begun talking I couldn't stop and I was practically on my knees begging for help. After I had finished spilling out my feelings, the doctor diagnosed me with depression and anxiety. He explained that it was triggered by the bereavement of my mother. Now I am fully aware which one of us had the medical degree, but I was offended when he confirmed what I already knew. I knew I was depressed and trust me I was well aware I had anxiety (it's not something you don't know you have.) If I wasn't so broken, I would have laughed in his face at his diagnosis because I didn't need him to point out the obvious. What I needed was help with it, that's what I knew nothing about. I had no idea what I should do and how to handle these feelings.

It made sense to me now why people with depression and anxiety want to sleep so much. It's the only time you don't feel useless and lost. It's a break away from the battle conversations happening in your head. Fighting with wanting to go outside and enjoy the fresh air, to having crippling fear about getting out of bed. I would convince myself that people would see my sadness and that it was easier to stay home (at least I wouldn't have to pretend that I was OK.) It's easier to hide away with your problems and ignore their existence, but it sure isn't the answer. It makes the healing process a great deal more difficult as well.

I knew walking through the surgery doors that I would be leaving with a prescription for antidepressants. When the doctor confirmed that I was depressed, there was absolutely no way I was leaving without that prescription. All I heard was my mum's voice protesting how useless and addictive they are, so I bit the bullet and told the doctor my concerns. I told him I didn't want to become reliant on the tablets. He actually looked at me as if I was crazy and then inhaled a breath (more than likely swallowing the frustration, he clearly knew the stigma.)

"Miss Price you'll only become addicted and dependant on medication, if you don't use it correctly or follow the recommended instructions. You will be given a course of tablets for three months but you're required to have a follow up appointment in a month. Then we will assess if the dose can be lowered." Although his explanation was a little 'salty' and 'passive aggressive,' I did feel assured. I could still hear mum's disapproval in my head and I could only imagine what her reaction would have been, seeing me with a box of happy pills.

The doctor advised me that depression could not be fixed quickly and that the tablets were a quick fix so he advised me to look at therapy too. He recommended that I should consult a therapist who is trained in bereavement counselling. Great... now I felt crazy, I wouldn't only be taking happy pills, I'd be sat across from a therapist.

Another mental health stigma perpetuated from a lack of understanding and stereotypical assumptions. Yet they manage to attach themselves as logical and rationalised theories in everyone's lives. I've only ever seen a therapy session in a film or TV programme, and the person who needed help was either dangerous to themselves or to others. *Why can't true representations of what these stigmas' hide be shown? Why does someone who needs therapy have to be conveyed as crazy?*

I didn't feel like I needed all of this 'help' and I felt it was over the top and unnecessary if I'm totally honest. I wanted a way out of the darkness and I assumed the answer would be easier and quicker than all the palaver I was given. Depression and especially grief doesn't have the easy way out button. Grief is the continuous pain from mourning someone who has been ripped from your life. Grief is the result of losing a person who you don't want to live without. My person was the woman who gave birth to me, the woman who had raised me and the woman who I shared unconditional love with. My person I was grieving was my mother.

Her death exploded my entire world apart and this process was going to be a massive battle and a really painful one too. It was and still is a battle that haunts me and it doesn't matter how much time passes, my world and life will never be the same again. Regardless how pointless I thought therapy and tablets were, I swallowed my fears and my doubts, because I was desperate for help. I was drowning in the rubble of my life and anything other than this suffering was going to be better. I left the doctors surgery with a battle plan nevertheless, even if I didn't see it that way at the time. I thought that after taking that first step that I would feel better. I knew I wasn't going to be immediately fixed or completely healed but I thought I would have felt lighter. Unfortunately that couldn't have been further from the truth. I walked out the surgery with the same sad and depressing feelings I had when I first arrived. Nothing had been lifted and I didn't have any relief, if anything I felt more pressure on my shoulders. I had more pain in my heart and more confusion in my mind. I had been given resources to help make me better and to possibly fix me, so the fear of it not working, terrified the life out of me.

I began to hate the person I was, I hated the pain I felt on a daily basis, the thoughts that spun my mind into panic and sadness. I hated every aspect of my life because I hated that I had a life when my mother did not and I despised people who still had their mothers. I had so much hatred inside of me that the memories of how and who I was before all of this, started to fade away. I was petrified that this was it for me, that this was who I had become and who I was destined to be. *What if this was my purpose?* I was scared that I was lost in this sea of poisoned hatred. I was being attacked by waves of sadness, currents of hatred and gallons of pain daily. It felt like I had no hope of being able to swim back to normality.

What if everything I heard and believed growing up is right? What if these tablets don't work? What if I'm not the right kind of mentally ill? Is therapy going to be a waste of time? What if this is it? What is this is who I will always be?

My fears were all born from my learned behaviours. Everything I had heard, seen and believed as a child was now tearing me apart. The good thing about learned behaviours are regardless of how ingrained they may be, you can unlearn them if you're willing and open-minded enough. It helped me that I had no other alternative, so I had to let go of my learned behaviours and gave the tablets a chance. I threw myself into those unknown waters and after taking the tablets for a few weeks I did feel different. I know I wasn't cured and I wasn't anywhere close to being fixed but I felt and noticed a difference. I had a small glimmer of my old self and she was fighting her way through the barriers.

Now as wonderful as the slight improvement was, the side effects were utterly horrendous. At the start I couldn't sleep at all and would be restless most of the night. Only to then feel sleepy throughout the whole day. My stomach was ridiculously upset too (not the most glamorous time of my life,) I became best friends with most toilets. My appetite had completely vanished and I lost weight (which believe me is never an issue, I have plenty to lose.) At this point, I could have given up and stopped the tablets but I persevered with the side effects. Even if some of them were a complete pain in my arse (some quite literally,) my head space had become lighter, and my thoughts didn't race through my brain at one hundred miles per hour anymore. I was given a break from my thoughts and I had time to process them. My mind was given a much needed top up of serotonin and I could smile again and not have to fake it.

I had to take one tablet per day and I began taking them in the morning before work, but they made me feel sick all the time. I couldn't focus properly and due to wanting to sleep all the time, I decided to take the tablet at night. At least if they made me feel sick, I would be at home. It did seem to help and thankfully my sleep pattern restored and I was sleeping for a decent amount of hours. I was roughly getting between five and six hours a night, I mean it was broken and not consecutive but nevertheless I was sleeping again.

Depression is a result of a physical imbalance within our brains. Our nerve cells produce serotonin and although it's mainly found in the digestive system, it also helps different parts of the brain to communicate with each other. It affects the brain cells relating to our mood, appetite, sleep, memory and social behaviour (please don't think I am medically trained, Google is just a wonderful service.) When we experience trauma, our serotonin levels decrease and our moods do not regulate efficiently. Therefore a person is more susceptible to depression if they have low serotonin.

Antidepressants are designed to increase the serotonin levels that are lacking in the body. The tablets will enable that person's moods to regulate more effectively and this is why they're often referred to as the 'quick fix.' People will begin to feel better and then make the grand old mistake of stopping the medication. As soon as this happens they fall back into their low moods and forget the reason why they needed tablets in the first place.

A traumatic experience will always be inside of you, it wraps around our hearts and it becomes ingrained into our minds. In order to heal the trauma we need to deal with it and that's why therapy is perfect (regardless how deep we may have buried it.) It is distressing and tough but trauma shouldn't be allowed to fester inside of you. It needs to be released and unlocked, in order for you to be free from its control. Nobody wants to sit across from a stranger and open up their world to them, especially when it's filled with pain. However the alternative is living with it daily and that is much more distressing. We always have a choice and sometimes it really is as simple as choosing what you want.

I know how scary it is to take that leap of faith and ask for help. It's hard and you will be crippled by fear but you need to remember how strong you are. You may feel the weakest you've ever felt in your life, you may feel worthless and you may feel like you can't do it but you can. You're not weak for asking for help, it's one of the strongest things you can ever do. To admit you're struggling takes a big pair of balls. Remaining quiet and struggling in silence is also strength just a different kind. To plaster over the cracks that are tearing you apart and pretending everything is ok, takes a whole world of strength. Regardless whether you reach out and share your struggles, or stay battling alone, remember you are worthy! Every person on this planet is worthy: worthy of help, happiness, love, respect and more importantly we're all worthy of life. You've got this and you can do it but it'll only work if you fight for it.

I fought and I fought hard. I had tried fighting in silence but I knew I needed help. I wanted to be a normal person again. I wanted the terrorising thoughts and pain that controlled my life to stop. My mother was never coming back, I had eternally lost her in this lifetime and I was getting far too close to losing myself.

I continued with my happy pills and they were working but I still felt incredibly sad and empty. I was deeply depressed and I needed something with longevity that would help me carry the aching pain. I have this pain for the rest of my life, so I needed much more than happy pills... I needed and more importantly, I wanted therapy.

Chapter Nineteen – Hitting Rock Bottom

The decision that I needed therapy was a difficult one to make. It was more difficult than making the initial doctor's appointment because I was placing myself into completely unknown territory. The only understanding I had about therapy was how films and television represented it. The idea of sitting with a complete stranger whilst they took notes on everything I said or did, had the hairs on my neck standing to attention. Allowing a stranger to listen to your darkest thoughts rippled fear throughout my body, and I felt physically sick.

My anxiety became more severe and my whole body felt cramped and locked. My hands felt sweaty and I had bitten my fingernails so far down that the skin was torn and bleeding. As sadistic as it sounds the pain from the opened skin gave me a sense of relief. My fingers were sore and offered me a newer feeling of pain. I struggled with getting my head around all of the changes happening. I had never experienced anxiety prior to all of this and I couldn't understand what was happening inside my head. I couldn't handle the thoughts and feelings, I had no strategy plan and I felt like I was in a losing battle. Anxiety really invades who you are and manipulates your normality. I knew I was overthinking everything, but I couldn't do anything to stop.

At my most anxious times my senses became heightened, and I was extremely sensitive and vulnerable to things that would normally be oblivious to me. Sound was the most challenging for me to persevere with and there were times I would hear each inhale a person took. It didn't matter the volume because everything sounded so deafeningly loud to me. Not only did I have sensitivity to outside noises, I also had to deal with my obnoxious inner dialogue. Internally I was listing every possible outcome for everything and it didn't matter how obscene and ridiculous they were, my anxiety made me believe they were realistic.

With my anxiety at an all-time high, I was convinced that therapy wasn't the answer and I shouldn't get help, *I was already judging and analysing myself enough, I didn't need a complete stranger to do it too.* They would write me off as crazy because they didn't know how I was feeling (once again my anxiety exceeding its purpose and objective.) Questions upon questions were thrown around my head and they shattered any hope I had. *What if this is something bigger than depression? What if this is something much worse? What if I am actually crazy? What if I need something bigger than therapy? What if I need to be sectioned? What if I am beyond help?* All of these 'what if' questions never stopped.

Today I see that I was in a state of panic and it was totally fuelled by anxiety and fear of the unknown. The stigma associated with therapy was all I had as a reference of what to expect, and with the thoughts I was having I thought it was true. Therapy is for the plain mad and back then, I felt completely and utterly insane. I was losing my mind, and every aspect of the person I once was, was shrinking every day. I couldn't recognise the person who looked back at me in the mirror.

The anger inside of me was starting to mount and I still wanted to punch random people in the face. I lost my temper at the slightest inconvenience and if I didn't want to talk (which was most of the time,) when somebody started a conversation, my response was either one worded, or I would just completely ignore them. I would sigh loud enough so it obvious. I was annoyed at the smallest attempt of interaction. Anytime it was suggested that I should go out and do something, I would shoot the idea down. I never had an excuse for not wanting to, I would simply refuse.

Traits that made me likable before this were now replaced with venom and poison, and I accepted it. I accepted it so quickly and comfortably because I was self-destructing and I was content with the person I had become. Nothing anybody said or tried to do had an impact, frankly I saw it as that I was right and everyone else was wrong. I was pushed everyone away who I wanted and needed and I knew it was wrong but I didn't care. I wanted to physically be alone so that the loneliness I felt inside made sense.

The fear of having therapy was because I knew I would have to talk about everything. Although I wanted to get every thought and emotion out and not bottle them up any longer, they were the only things I had that made me feel close to my mum. I wanted to tell everyone exactly how I was feeling and at times it was on the tip of my tongue, but I bit my tongue and I pushed them all back down. I forced them back into my volt of silence. *Did it help to be silent? Was it easier to suffer in silence?*

I can categorically say there is nothing easy about suffering and staying silent. Not verbally sharing how you're feeling doesn't make you silent. You may not have verbalised it to others, but you still hear and feel it. There is nothing silent about suffering it's the loudest noise you'll ever make. Those with the slightest level of emotional intelligence won't need you to say you're suffering because everything else you do will tell them. They will notice how many times you excuse yourself from every invite. They will notice how your appetite changes. They will notice how certain things no longer make you smile. People will notice all these things over and over again and still not let you know they are aware.

They won't do anything because you'll just tell them 'I'm fine' each time they ask you. I know this because I did it to all the people who noticed the changes in me. I didn't want anyone who I cared about to worry, or know how deeply sad I *really* was. They didn't need to know how much pain my heart was actually in, and they didn't need to know how much torture my mind was dealing with. I didn't want to be a burden and make the relationships awkward because if they truly knew, they wouldn't know what to say or how to handle it. Everyone would treat me as if I was going to break and they would all walk on egg shells around me.

If only I could have seen at the time that they were already doing that. People avoided doing or saying anything that made me sad or angry. They were already walking on eggshells each time they were around me because they were completely aware of how broken I was. It was me who was oblivious, I couldn't see how broken I was, and the only person I was pretending to be fine around was myself.

I felt unbearable pressure on a daily basis and I didn't have the energy anymore to suppress my thoughts and feelings. I felt them boil dangerously high and I knew that at any given moment they would spill over. The sadness controlled every aspect of my life and slowly I was losing the fight with myself. I needed to talk and I wanted to talk. I wanted to be better and to feel normal again... I wanted to be me again. That's when I decided I would give therapy a chance because I couldn't fight anymore: I was tired. I needed to be helped out my of darkness so I dialled the number for the bereavement counsellor.

My anxiety gripped me tighter with every unanswered ring and my thumb hovered over the cancel button, with the anticipation of hearing another voice. I was sweating and my forehead was damp. If I had to wait a second longer, I would have pressed the big red cancel button but then I heard a voice.

"Hello Cruise Bereavement how can I help?" *Well it was now or never. I'm still surprised to this day, how my first word's on that call wasn't explicit.* I explained that I had been referred by my doctor and then gave the reasons why I found myself needing help. I told them I was grieving my mother and how the hole within my world was swallowing me up. As soon as I had explained everything I felt a sigh leave my mouth, and I felt the ripple of relief throughout my body. Thoughts I had been bottling up were now out in the open and it felt good. Of course I knew I wasn't fixed after talking to a telephone operator: in fact, as lovely and helpful as she was, she actually infuriated me. Throughout the entire call I could feel her sympathy head tilt. *Why do people do that?*

When someone hears other people's bad news, they tilt their head to one side and then look at you with puppy dog eyes. Their voices become an inch off being patronising and you can almost taste their pity. I hated it because I was fully aware of how sad my situation was. I was aware of how gut wrenching it was because I lived it every day, so the last thing I needed was to be reminded how devastating my life had become. Thankfully the call wasn't long and I only had to endure the sympathy for a short while. I was added to their waiting list and would be contacted as soon as possible, as the next stage was a telephone assessment with a trained councillor.

I was astounded that I was added to a list and not seen straight away if I'm honest. However the more you learn about mental health, it becomes apparent how underfunded it is. I have a very small understanding of politics but I do think health care should be free and accessible for everyone. Health is a basic human right and there should never be a price attached to getting help with it; physical or mental and certainly not a waiting list.

All I could do was sit tight and wait for someone to find my name on a list, and decide if I was worth a telephone assessment. That's probably not the reality of how the process works, but it felt that way. In my mind I was a perfect fit for bereavement counselling, I was mourning the death of my mother and I was going out of my *fucking* mind. A perfect candidate if you had of asked me (I got my vote.) Waiting a few more days, weeks or possibly months was nothing: I had already endured hell for four months. *My situation was already bad so how much worse could it possibly get?*

In short…it got worse. Never believe things can't get any worse than they may already be because they can get a whole world worse. I was really struggling now and my mind was only occupied with sad thoughts. Every day I felt close to bursting into tears and nothing even needed to happen, I was emotional all the time. I would often wake up with a wet face from crying. It wasn't just within my conscious state I was sad, I was even sad in my sleep.

My mind insisted that it needed to remind me I no longer had a mother on minute by minute basis. This thought and realisation will always drench my heart with pain and make my eyes buckle from tears. The fact I will never get to see my mum again is the most painful, lonely and gut wrenching feeling I've ever experienced. No matter how much time passes, losing a parent will always rip your heart into shreds. There are times that all I need and want is my mum, and knowing I can't ever have that only makes me need and want it more.

I found that everything reminded me of her and I would imagine what she would have said or done in situations. I would remember all the times my stomach ached from laughing at her and I would randomly smell her perfume. I was trapped inside this wheel of everlasting torture and I was ready to give up. I had become empty inside and completely numb, I couldn't feel anything other than despair. It felt as if I had been plunged into ice water and my body froze from the outside in.

There was only one other time I had felt similar and that was when I was at school. I would always be so nervous before exams that I would be physically sick in the morning. I can't remember the exact exam it was, but I had this exact feeling of complete numbness and emptiness. A teacher noticed and handed me an elastic band, and told me whenever they felt nervous, they would ping an elastic band against their wrist. Apparently the shock and the abruptness of pain gave their brain a break from the panic and calmed them down.

Firstly I do not advise this as a coping mechanism at all so please don't try it! However I remember doing this every time I had an exam (even at University.) So when I began having these feelings of numbness again, I remembered this technique and started to wear an elastic band. I started to wear one at work and each time I felt anxious, I would ping the band against the inside of my wrist. It only started with being an occasional ping at first and sometimes I would ping too hard that I had to take the band off. However like any habit it started becoming more regular and I got so used to it I wouldn't take the band off until I came home. I didn't realise how reliant I had become until one particular day.

I woke up after having yet another poor night's sleep and went to work (so far nothing out of the ordinary.) I felt different this particular morning and I had a sinking feeling inside. My grief felt heavier this day and I couldn't seem to shake it off. Refusing to explain this to my manager (who would have probably allowed me to have the day off,) I stayed silent. If I'm being honest I didn't want to be alone. I was becoming scared of being alone now, I wouldn't say I was *suicidal* or anything, but I didn't care if something would have happened to me. I wouldn't have actively tried to take my own life, but I didn't have much enthusiasm to live either. It's hard to articulate because I wasn't suicidal but I did have suicidal thoughts. Anyway I grabbed an elastic band from my box and placed it around my wrist. I had used these bands so much that they no longer gave me relief and it was now a habit. I had stopped feeling the pings against my wrist and was numb to the pain it caused, because I had done it so much. However the feeling of the final ping I ever made against my wrist on this day, I will always remember.

After I had pulled the band back and it slapped around my wrist, I was met with a chillingly numb sensation. It wasn't something I had felt from them before and it felt like I had cut open my skin. My wrist trickled with coldness and I instantly knew I had fucked up. I didn't want to look down at my wrist, I felt embarrassed and ashamed because I wasn't this person. I tucked my wrist under my sleeve, expecting it to stick to the blood I thought was there, and walked as fast as I could to the toilets. I pushed down the toilet seat, took a deep breath and sat down. I tore off some toilet tissue (still refusing to even look at my wrist,) closed my eyes and wrapped the tissue around my wrist. Nothing...I had braced myself to feel a sting, to feel instant pain but...I felt nothing. I only felt pressure under my skin, as if I was pressing on the skin inside my arm. I opened my eyes and removed the tissue exposing my wrist and I felt like I had been kicked in the stomach by Big Foot.

As I stared at my wrist, tears spilt down my face because I was so ashamed and embarrassed with myself. I had used the elastic band so much and with too much force that, my skin had a deep and thick purple-black bruise wrapped around it. I traced my finger across the bruise and the sensation didn't resonate in my brain. I had bruised it so deep that there was no feeling to the skin. That was the moment I knew I had gone too far. I had totally lost every inch of who I was. I stood up and looked at myself in the mirror that was in the toilet and I cried even harder. I didn't see myself...I saw a completely broken shell of a human being. It was the sadness in the reflection that stared back that made me that made me cry harder. I was crying for the person I saw because they were begging for help and I pitted them.

That saddest part was the broken and desperate person crying for help, was me. I really needed help and I wanted someone to take this pain away because I couldn't handle it anymore. I wasn't physically strong enough to carry this grief anymore. I was weak in every way: physically, emotionally and mentally. I had hit my rock bottom and I smacked every rock on the way down. I was lying amongst the rubble of my shattered life when I received the call I had been waiting for.

Chapter Twenty – Therapy Thursdays

It was two weeks since I had taken the leap of faith and called the number for bereavement counselling. I had become an even sadder existence than I thought was imaginable. I had continued taking my happy pills and they were working to an extent, but they simply weren't enough. It was also a week after my shameful experience with the elastic band strategy and I continued to feel emptiness in my heart and soul. I had no purpose or enthusiasm to wake up in the morning and I felt like an imposter living someone else's life. However I received a call whilst at work to have my pre-counselling assessment (basically a call to see how depressed I was and at what urgency I needed help.) The questions were probing and uncomfortable.

It was near impossible to explain to a stranger that I didn't feel suicidal, but I also didn't have the enthusiasm to live either. It was also extremely exhausting trying not to burst out crying with every answer, and to not sound as depressed as I felt. I'm happy to announce…I passed my assessment (yay!) Normally I would have been happy to pass a test but this time around, I didn't have that satisfaction feeling. Instead I had an abundance of sickening and painful anxiety. I had proved that I needed professional help with my mental health and that made me feel like I was classified as crazy. I was now going to be sat face-to-face with a counsellor whilst they score that craziness (how wonderful.)

I would be lying if I said I wasn't relieved though, I could share all this weight I had carried on my shoulders for the past four months. Someone else was about to hear what I had been hiding inside for all that time. I finally had a source of help and a window in my caged box of concrete walls. I had been given my flash of light and hope in my darkened world. At the end of my assessment I was told my first session was booked in for the following Thursday at six o'clock in the evening.

The week that led up to my first session was filled with apprehension and questions. I told my dad and my friends that I was struggling with my grief, and had organised professional help. They never said, but I assume that they were probably more relieved than I was, (they must have been sick and tired of walking on eggshells around me.)

I was so deep into my depression that I hadn't realised how selfish I had become. I was too selfish that I had forgotten my dad was also grieving, he was grieving the same person I was but to him, she was someone different. I was grieving my mother, the woman who gave birth to me and the woman who gave me life, but dad was grieving his soul mate. He was mourning the woman he was deeply in love with and his other half. My dad had lost the woman who brought his daughter into this world, and gave his life a new purpose. There wasn't one moment I stopped to think, even worse, asked how he was feeling or coping. I was so wrapped up in my own misery that I failed to see how distraught my own father was. Grief made me oblivious to anyone else's pain and suffering because the torture in my own mind isolated me from everything and everyone. All I knew was how *I* felt and what *I* was thinking.

If you've done the same or are doing the same, my only advice is to not feel bad. You're not neglecting anyone on purpose, you're simply being swamped by your own mind and body. People will not hold it against you because they understand more than you think they do. If anyone refuses to understand then I would advise analysing your support network. A quote from Nipsey Hussle says it perfectly: *"If you look at the people in your circle and don't get inspired, then you don't have a circle you have a cage."* You shouldn't be made to feel judged, uninspired or trapped in your circle. Your support network doesn't have to agree with you all the time but they should always understand and support you no matter what.

Although it's not your fault that you neglect others while dealing with your turmoil, it becomes a choice the moment you notice how you're behaving. If you notice the neglect you're doing and continue doing it with consciousness, you can no longer use it as an excuse. For me, my realisation came after I had organised therapy and now I had a choice to either take the help or give into the voice of doubt in my head. I had a choice to make a change and it was no longer just for the benefit of myself, it was also now for the benefit of others. If I took the help and went to therapy, my dad could deal with his own grief, rather than consistently focus on making sure I was OK.

Thursday had raced around quickly and before I knew it I was on my way to the Wisdom hospice in Rochester, Kent, for my first counselling session. This is the ugly beauty of life because I was going to a hospice, for a second chance at life, whilst others were being made as comfortable as possible in the lead up to the end of their lives. As I walked up to the entrance of the hospice, I felt the anxiety pulsate through my body harder than my heartbeat. The reality of what I was just about to walk into hit me like a brick. I felt unbelievably vulnerable and I was completely stripped of protection. I made an attempt to release the tension in my hands by cracking my knuckles but it failed, instead they remained tight as stone.

Every fibre of my body wanted to turn back around and forget the whole thing. So I closed my eyes and I took in a deep breath, releasing it slowly and reminding myself why I was there. Although I may not have wanted to do it, I desperately needed to and despite wanting to, I was not going to turn around and chicken out on this. I owed it to myself, I had suffered enough and I deserved peace. Whilst I battled with my inner voice and fear, my feet had carried me to the front desk and I had no choice now but to sign myself in. After I added my name in the security book, I was shown through to their kitchen area and told someone would come and collect me. I was also told to help myself to tea and coffee, but that was the last thing on my mind. I just wanted to be home and for this to all be over with. I don't recall exactly how long I was waiting for but it felt like an eternity.

My exterior silence and inner panic was interrupted by an older woman. She stood in front of me with her arm extended ready to shake my hand. The woman was around 5.6'in height and appeared to be in her forties (I hope.) Her face wore a friendly smile; it was different to the ones I was used to. It was a genuine smile and it was absent of sympathy and pity. I stood up, greeted her handshake and then she introduced herself. "Hello my name is Dawn. You must be Jade... it's nice to meet you. If you follow me we can get started."

It was only then that I appreciated the length of time I was waiting for. This was the moment I had been anticipating and it was now or never. It felt like someone had hit the fast-forward button and I was following Dawn's lead. Before my brain could catch up, I was walking through the door to the room where I spent the next hour. I don't know what I was expecting, but the room was different to what I had thought it would be. It was just a normal room, there wasn't a chaise longue, any sofa or coffee table, no plants and it wasn't dark.

There were two wooden framed chairs facing each other, with a dull pink fabric wrapped around the seated cushion. To the side of one of the chairs was a small wooden table, and around the edges of the room were, unused chairs positioned side by side. Sunlight was blasted around which made the room brighter than I had expected. I guess I was imagining the rooms that TV and film portrayed and I was relieved that it was nothing like that.

I took my seat with my back towards the window, facing the door and I became instantly aware of my body language. Inside of my head I wanted to sit with my knees up to my chin, with my arms wrapped around my legs for extra protection. I didn't want to be an open book and I didn't want to be vulnerable. I wanted to protect myself, my thoughts and my feelings. I didn't want to let anyone in because this was my struggle. I thought that if I let someone know exactly what was going on inside of me and inside of my head, I wouldn't be strong anymore. I would be completely out of control and weak.

Even though that's how I wanted to be positioned I decided not to. I sat with my feet firmly attached to the floor and consciously placed my arms across the arms of the chair, wrapping my palms around the edges. I wanted to look as open as possible but I have no idea why (I was even overthinking this part of the session.) If anything, it was going to be picked up that my body language looked utterly false. I had gripped onto the edges of the chair so hard that my knuckles wore a blanket of white skin. My entire body was stiff and the more I tried to hide it, the more obvious it became.

The distance between the two chairs wasn't an issue, until Dawn took her position in the one facing me. When we were sat directly opposite each other, I noticed how close the chairs were. If I had stretched my leg out, I would have kicked her shin. This new intimate setting was another element that I had to digest. Considering I was going to be opening the door to my grief and depressive demon, being this close with a complete stranger was quite intimidating. I wanted to push my legs back forcing more distance but it was too late. We both got as comfortable as possible and Dawn began the session. *This is it. Basically I will be sat on this strangers lap for a whole, entire hour...fantastic Jade!*

As the session started I was informed about the rules of confidentiality. Everything we discussed would stay between the two of us, with exceptions, of course. I was told that it would need to be reported if I posed a threat to myself or someone else, if I was selling drugs or even more extreme... if I was involved in any terrorist activities (what the hell?)

Now thankfully I didn't need to worry about any of these scenarios, because none of them applied. However it made me wonder how powerful these sessions could be. If people have admitted to being involved in terrorist activity, this should be a breeze for me. After all, I was only hiding my grief, not the fact I was a terrorist. To be honest, all sarcasm aside, I was left thinking about how deep these sessions were going to go and it petrified me. I didn't know the extent of my grief and how badly it had affected me. *What if Dawn actually discovers I am, in fact, crazy?*

Spoiler alert...I wasn't shown any pictures of weird shapes and asked what the first thing I thought of was (I know I was disappointed a little too!) Therapy really wasn't what I had perceived it to be. Yes it was exposing and it left me completely open, but it was actually quite nice to get all your harboured thoughts and feelings out. I relished in the ability to talk without the fear of burdening someone I loved or being judged. For the very first time since mum had died, I had answered honestly to how I was feeling. I no longer needed to hold back for the sake of someone else's feelings, and I could be as brutal as I wanted to be. As much as it was liberating, I was still crippled with fear. Each time Dawn spoke I held onto my breath making my body tense the whole time.

"How are you?" This was Dawn's first question and it was simple yet triggering. After releasing the breath I was keeping hostage, I closed my eyes to compose myself. I was not ready to cry in front of this stranger. With a tremble in my voice I confessed "I'm sad, I just feel sad." I had no other way of expressing how I felt, and all that I could recognise was the overwhelming feeling of sadness. I was engulfed in agonising sadness and it hurt: physically, mentally and emotionally, it hurt. All I had felt in every second, every minute, every hour, every day and every week since she had died, was sadness.

Unveiling how I felt unlocked the gates that protected all of my feelings and thoughts and soon enough, I was recalling the day mum died. I was reliving the day my whole world changed, when my normality died along with the person I once was. I don't know how or why but, that one simple question led me to talk for a solid half an hour. I had spent half of my first session simply offloading and Dawn never stopped me once. She let me offload, hurt and cry, she allowed me space and time to simply feel. I instantly felt my chest loosen and it no longer felt claustrophobically tight. My shoulders didn't feel like they were carrying the weight of my world either. Did I feel better? Absolutely and categorically no, I did not, I did not feel better... let me be clear I was not fixed, I was still very much broken. However, for the very first time; whilst I was still drowning in my mental instability, I could breathe again without the air getting stuck in my throat.

I hadn't even touched upon the depths of how I was feeling. Feeling sad was the neat and tidy package I used to present a whole host of feelings and emotions. How could I explain without sounding crazy, that I was empty inside yet completely full of emotions? How could I explain that, despite being conscious to the abundance of pain I was in, I still felt completely lost and utterly numb? How could I explain that I was so exhausted but couldn't sleep? How could I explain how disturbingly angry I was, yet desperately vulnerable? How could I explain that all I wanted was to be cuddled until my heart no longer ached, but I didn't want to be around people? How could I explain that I felt lonely, yet entirely smothered by everyone and everything?

Physically I may have felt lighter but mentally and emotionally, I had never felt heavier. The session came to an end and after a quick discussion about next week's agenda, and if I wanted to continue the sessions (yes I did,) I made my way home. When I stepped outside and the fresh air had hit me, I felt every ounce of pain that I managed to block out. My heart felt sore it no longer ached or hurt, it was sore, and I felt the pain in every single part of my body. All I wanted to do was to be at home in a bath, but at the same time I wanted to walk until I felt no more pain. I hadn't spoken about how I felt until now, especially about the day that haunted my every thought. I had relived the day my mother was ripped out of my world. I had recalled the whole thing out loud and I hadn't realised how much harder it was to talk about the day, than it was to see it in my mind constantly. Saying it out loud meant I had to accept it had happened, it becomes real and it hits you. Oh boy did the reality hit me; it was like a pile of monster trucks smashing into me. I cried during the entire walk back home but not the ugly cry though... I know that you know the one, it's the cry that distorts your entire face and snot just produces quicker than you imagined was possible (thankfully it wasn't that cry!)

Tears flew down my face at the speed of light and nothing was stopping them, no matter how hard I tried. I don't know what exactly it was that I was crying for. Maybe it was the acknowledgement of finally telling someone how I felt, or maybe it was the fact I had relived mum's death out loud (maybe it was everything!) I finally felt sorry for myself and I don't mean that sarcastically. I recognised everything that had happened and I had connected with myself again and I really felt what I was going through. I know it sounds bizarre that I am speaking about myself as if I was someone else, but that's exactly how I felt. I was disconnected with myself and with the pain I felt. I couldn't connect to it because I desperately didn't want to acknowledge it. Now I had no alternative option, I was physically feeling everything that I had felt emotionally and mentally.

I think acknowledgement is actually the perfect description of what had happened. I of course was aware of what happened, I knew what had happened but I didn't want to acknowledge it. I didn't want to believe it, I couldn't face it, I didn't want to accept it, but after my session I was forced to believe, face and accept it.

I was glad to see my front door and I couldn't wait to just lie in a bath for hours, I was so drained (who knew walking and crying at the same time, would be such a strenuous task.) I knew that dad would want to know how my first session went, and I was prepared for the fact I would have to talk about it. As predicted dad asked how it went and I obliged in telling him, I've never hidden anything from him (well expect my internal suffering at the time,) so I was honest and we discussed how my first session went. That's the thing about opening up once you undo the lid, you no longer have control over holding it back anymore (it will come as no surprise that I slept like a baby that night.)

I was one session down and still had three sessions of 'Therapy Thursday's' to come. It was going to be a very draining and emotionally stretching month.

Chapter Twenty-One – Therapy Thursdays Part II

My therapy sessions were scheduled every Thursday at 6pm for an entire month. Each session was an hour long it was the most draining yet refreshing experience I've ever endured. It's a strange sense of relief to speak to a stranger about your deep, dark thoughts and feelings. The ability to offload the emotions that keep you awake at night, and contort your body into a rigid frame of anxiety, felt like freedom.

In the beginning I hated the idea of sitting with a stranger for a whole hour, to share what was haunting my life. I feared that what I said would be twisted, to fit me into the crazy box. I was scared of the unknown because I didn't know what the therapist would be thinking, writing and concluding about me. I was powerless to their judgement and I had no control over the outcome of my sessions. The judgment from everyone else also terrified me because I grew up believing people with mental health problems were crazy. The tables had turned and I was now the one seeking professional help and taking prescribed tablets because of my own mental state. *Isn't karma a bitch?*

During this time I was worried that people would judge me for being weak or crazy, and write me off as useless. I didn't want anyone to treat me as if I was too fragile to joke around with, too broken to confide in and too risky to upset. I knew I had changed and was different to how I was before, but I didn't want anyone to treat me differently. The person who I was before was still there but I was just hidden under a blanket of darkness and grief. Today is a different story because I truly do not care for anybody's judgement. People will have an opinion regardless of what you do, who you are and everything in between. The only person's judgement I am concerned for is my own.

Those fears of judgement would not prevent me getting professional help again if I need it. I now know that reaching out for help is not a sign of weakness; it's actually the purest form of strength that exists. To place your vulnerability, insecurities and trust into someone else's hands takes courage. It takes guts, bravery, resilience and a good set of steel balls. At the time I was ashamed that I had to rely on a stranger for help, but I'm so proud of myself that I did. I helped myself more than anybody else could have, by seeking professional help when I needed it.

I told someone I'm close to that I was having counselling sessions and their response knocked me for six. I had built up the courage to admit to them that I was getting support with my mental health, and they simply replied: "Oh are you? That has shocked me, you're not as strong as I thought." I felt like I had been kicked in the stomach and my mind instantly began overthinking everything. I didn't expect that response and I didn't have the mind-set that I do today (I think they would have been the one knocked for six.) Instead I was fighting with the voices inside my head who were now telling me that I should be stronger. *Should I be dealing with this on my own? Am I just weak and this is why I felt the way I do?*

The truth was I was weak and I felt weak. I didn't have the strength to continuously suffer the pain I was dealing with, that is why I needed help. I no longer wanted to fake a smile when all I wanted to do was cry. I didn't want to worry about my dad being on his own because something might happen and I wouldn't be there. I was exhausted of fighting on my own and if that made me weak...I'm happy with that. I needed someone to help me out of this dark, swallowing hole I was in. I needed a hand to grip on to and to help pull me out of it. I wasn't going to get that help from anyone around me because I wasn't going to burden those I cared about.

I don't hold anything against the person who said what they did and I never would. I'm still close to them today because they were entitled to an opinion and they have their own beliefs. I understood their opinion, it was formed from the same beliefs I had growing up. It's not about who was wrong or right in the situation, but to have the rights to an opinion you must be rightly informed. There is no harm in asking some questions to get clarity, before making an assumption that may or may not be correct.

This is why it's so important to raise awareness of the stigma attached to mental health. The stigmas around mental health and those who are affected by it are damaging. When we allow them to exist, people who need help will be too ashamed and afraid of getting it. Society has taught us all different conceptions of what 'perfect' is and what it should look like. All of the conceptions are unattainable and are simply fantasy. We must remember that a concept is an idea, and not fact: it is a method of projecting a desirable truth but not an essential one. Every single person on this planet will have a different concept of perfect and we all should, because we are all different versions of perfect. The problems stem when people try to force their conception of perfection into others lives.

Mental health is not a concept and it's not based on opinions. It's not something a person strives to have and nobody makes a choice to have it. There isn't a website or shop that sells different conditions. Mental health is a physical condition, a physical attribute of someone's personality, just like someone's sexual preference and someone's skin colour. It doesn't define them and it's not everything that they are, it is only a *part* of the person that they are. Thankfully it's no longer acceptable to judge people based on their sexual preference or skin colour, so why is it perfectly acceptable to judge someone's mental health?

It has taken years and years to re-educate generations that it doesn't make a person any less perfect if they have a different colour skin and a different cultural background to the white race. It has also taken years to teach generations that, those within the LGBTQ+ community are just as perfect as straight Karen from the local church. It has taken decades to get to the stage we're at right now and yet there are still bigoted opinions that bring hate onto people.

What I'm trying to say, which I could have summed up in a sentence (but hey I'm writing a book,) is someone will always have something to say. However every stigma and prejudice opinion needs to be re-educated and called out. We cannot allow other people's ignorance to affect our lives and certainly not our health. We all have the power to change what is acceptable, and we all know right from wrong. If you have no logical or structured reason to judge or hold an opinion then you need to educate yourself to widen your understanding.

Once again I digress... reaching out and asking for that help was one of the best things I ever did. It gave me more strength and I needed it to continue fighting my grief. I will always be grateful for therapy. I had the power to change what was no longer acceptable for me and I would chose to do it over and over again.

I only had a total of four hours of therapy and in the beginning I didn't think it would be enough. How could I be fixed in four hours, considering I had been in this state for months? That was lesson number one: *therapy doesn't fix you.* No, it's not a paradox; therapy simply gives you all you need to fix yourself. The four sessions I had gave me the opportunity to talk openly and honestly, about how I was feeling and what I was thinking. I released some of my negative energy that I had harboured up. I had a safe place to speak about everything and I was given advice and coping mechanisms that I could use too. I had a professional counsellor who made sense of the way I felt and that was all I needed.

I understood what my trigger points were and when they were likely to happen. Having that knowledge helped me prepare for them and I could identify when my anxiety would be likely to strike. Although I could identify them, it didn't mean I could stop them from happening, but I was better equipped with dealing with them. I was no longer suffering and surrendering to their power, I could fight back. Therapy gave me the comfort of knowing it wasn't all me and it wasn't all in my head. It allowed me to accept it was ok to feel and think the way I did, and I realised very quickly that everything I was going through was *normal*.

Throughout my sessions I constantly compared how I used to be, to the person I had become and it became a trend. I heavily relied on the word *normal* to describe how I was before mum died. I made it clear that what I was currently feeling didn't feel normal to me. I was struggling to let go of my previous normality. Dawn asked in one of the sessions why I kept referring to the word *normal,* and what did it look like for me. There aren't many times when I am lost for words but this was one of them. The question stumped me and I had no answer, all I knew was how I felt before mum died and, how I felt after were worlds apart.

Normal to me represents a time when I was happy, able to socialise and have fun. *Normal* for me was when nothing affected me, and I didn't take anything personally. Normal for me was being able to see my mum, talk to her, warm her hands up when they were cold and laugh at her ridiculous sense of humour. Normal for me was when I had two living parents. That was the normality I couldn't let go of and it was what I desperately craved to go back to. Physically I was ripped away from my normality but I was still trapped emotionally. That version of normal for me no longer existed and I couldn't accept it, nor did I want to. Everything had changed, nothing was the same and it had all changed for the worse.

My new normal consisted of being scared of falling asleep because I was constantly plagued by flashbacks. I didn't enjoy anything about life anymore and I didn't want to be around people. I was snapping at every little thing people did because I was overly sensitive. I didn't see the fun in life anymore and I had nothing to smile about. My normal now meant I had just one living parent. My new normal hurt and it hurt like nothing I had felt before. I hated my new normal and I was refusing to accept it, but the problem was my new normal didn't care for how I felt. It wasn't going to change back and this was how my life was now, whether I liked it or not.

I have learnt that normality is never consistent. It never stays the same and what we perceive as normal changes all the time. That's why it is impossible to define because it's too ambiguous. What I consider normal another person would not, and what we feel is normal today may not be normal tomorrow. That was the biggest lesson I had to learn: I had to accept and realise the normality I once had no longer existed and would never return.

Though my normal had changed it didn't mean *I* wasn't normal, I could still be me. I had to find peace within myself to accept my new normality (of course this is all easier said than done.) It wasn't an overnight fix and I wasn't magically healed, I was still very low. Every day was a battle to face up to the loss I had both in my heart and in my life.Therapy had helped me enormously but it didn't offer me a solution and it didn't fix my broken pieces. That was my job, I had to fix myself and I had to put the work in to heal my own broken pieces.

I tried desperately hard to rebuild myself and make myself enjoy life again. I found it a little easier to talk to others about how I was feeling now, and I no longer had the urge to shut people out. I continued taking medication to help with my depression but I also started to meditate too. I tried to meditate when I felt too consumed with anxiety and depressive thoughts. I wouldn't say I was doing it correctly but it did help, it cleared my mind and gave me back control over my thoughts. I won't give false hope and pretend that it was all plain sailing, and that therapy had changed my life. I remained very much depressed and I was struggling more than I wanted to be. I endured moments where I didn't want to be around anyone, and I still had night terrors that stopped me sleeping. I cried in pain at the loss and emptiness I had in my heart most days and some would agree that I was still an absolute nightmare to be around.

My personality had changed and to be honest, today I am so grateful that it did. Ironically losing my mother made me gain a whole new perspective and attitude towards life. The changes were harder to accept back then because they felt ugly, but I have now grown to appreciate and love them. I was rude, selfish and I didn't care if I had upset anyone else. Admittedly these traits were obnoxious and toxic, but that is what I had become. Despite all the work I was doing I was still a bitch and I wasn't oblivious to it either, I knew when I was in one of those moods. It ruined relationships and although I am apologetic for any upset that I caused I do not have any regrets. I was evolving and adapting into my new normality, whilst trying to navigate through my grief journey. Unfortunately situations and people are not always meant to evolve with you, and that is exactly what happened. I can never regret who I was and I certainly am not ashamed of it because it was a part of my healing process.

I have changed the once ugly traits into some of my biggest strengths today. I no longer do everything I can, to make others happy. If something goes against my values and morals I won't accept it and I'll address it. I now love the traits that I once detested about me. I had to learn to love them because they weren't going away. I had changed as a person and all I had the power and control to do, was to develop these traits into strengths I could be proud of. The changes to my personality was a result of the journey I was forced on, and I had to accept that I couldn't 'just get over it,' I needed to address my pain and allow myself to be broken. Without this acceptance I would never be able to heal properly.

There's no use in pretending to be ok because it doesn't make anything go away and it certainly doesn't help you. My only advice is not to rush your journey and do not feel pressured into being ok. If you need to spend a day crying in bed, then you go and spend a day crying in bed. If you need to be angry, then you go be angry. You have to do what you need to in order to heal. However don't be an angry and rude arsehole for the sake of it. You need to be proactively helping yourself to heal, because otherwise your toxicity will eat you alive.

I discovered the ability to self-help when I started to write, it gave me a creative outlet for my emotions and thoughts. I had found an outlet for my mind to focus on something other than how sad I felt. I wrote exactly what I needed to at any time, and it became my healthy vice to run to. It was my natural medicine and my very own free therapy sessions. Without conscious acknowledgement, I began to rebuild myself because I was channelling all of my negative energy onto a page. Writing is my escape and it's my therapy and all you need to do is find yours.

Nevertheless I was far from finished with my journey and just when everything began to steady itself I hit a stumbling block. All of the healing I had worked on had come undone in a matter of seconds. It had taken months to get myself in a stable state of mind. I had enjoyed my birthday, Christmas and I even managed get through the first anniversary of mum's death. However I was one celebration away from hitting my truest rock bottom, and one celebration away from losing all hope of getting better. The day that tipped me over the edge, and I found myself free falling back into darkness was Mother's Day 2017.

Chapter Twenty-Two: The Year Of Firsts

After someone you love dies, you're not left to adjust in peace. Grief always manages to raise its ugly head, to give you reality checks and the hardest are the 'first times.' Facing important and meaningful days like anniversaries, birthdays and special occasions without them are the hardest. Within the same year of my mother dying, I had experienced ten first times and these were before the first year anniversary of her death.

I experienced my first mother's day without a mother and a father's day that reminded me, that I only had one living parent. I then had to celebrate dad's birthday, knowing that mum's was just fourteen days after. I had seven nieces and nephews' who would have their first birthdays without their nan. My brother and sister's had also had their first birthday's without our mother. Then I had my own experience of receiving my first birthday card not signed 'love from mum and dad' at the bottom.

Five days after my birthday was Christmas and it was the first one with one less present pile, one less plate at the table and one missing name on all of our presents. Christmas was the hardest 'first' because it's a time that's focused around family, yet we were adjusting to the missing piece in ours. Finally it was the first New Year without her. This one reinstalled the reality that I was entering a new year without my mum being alive. Not only that, it also meant the first year anniversary of her death was approaching too.

Although all of these firsts placed a huge amount of pressure on my mental health, I managed to get through them regardless. I was sad on each of them and I cried on most of them. I also hurt that bit more each time I faced one, but I got through them. I didn't expect how well I dealt with them and this made me believe I had turned a massive corner in my grief journey. I thought I was finally getting back to normal and was starting to accept this was how my life was. I thought how I felt during the 'first times' was completely normal, I didn't have that feeling of dread and I genuinely believed I had come full circle. I'd convinced myself that I could start moving on.

The only issue of course, was that I had completely fooled myself into a false sense of security. I had tricked myself into thinking that after one year I was better, and I thought I was healed. When in reality I was the complete opposite, I was just numb to the pain. I had subconsciously blocked out how much I was hurting. I wasn't dealing with anything, I hadn't turned a corner and I certainly hadn't accepted life without my mother. It had become apparent over Christmas that I was still struggling, especially when I began to write again. So many of the feelings that I believed were gone, were still festering away under the surface. I had subconsciously chosen not to acknowledge the gravity and significance of all the first times, and that's how I enabled myself to believe I had magically moved on. I had blocked out every emotion and feeling so much that I felt nothing and I confused that with being fixed.

When New Year introduced itself I had silently fallen back into a depressed state, but this time around I had mastered the art of pretending that everything was hunky dory. On the days when I couldn't disguise how I felt, I would pass it off as a bad day and nothing more. I pretended I was better and I was no longer wrapped up in darkness. However I was once again a complete mess, I was broken and falling to pieces inside. This pretence of growth and healing proceeded months into the New Year and before I knew it, it was the first year to the day mum had died. Yet again I was only upset on the outside at a limit I wanted people to know and see. I had now created this façade that I was better, so everything I decided to show was only surface level. Inside was a different story, I was shattering into a million pieces. I had the familiar thoughts of not wanting to be around anymore.

I was ashamed that I felt devastatingly low again after I had therapy and painfully bared my soul. I desperately tried to hold myself together but, I don't think the effort I made to put on a front, worked. I don't know if people saw through my fake happiness and false smiles, but what I do know was that I was exhausted. I was embarrassed that I had let myself down and allowed myself to fall back into depression again, but I was tired of fighting. I was sick of feeling and thinking the way I did and I was bored of the constant pain that paralysed my chest.

This time I knew I had a massive problem because it felt different, and I couldn't shake it off no matter how much I tried. The techniques I had learnt from therapy, meditating and journaling made no difference. I couldn't catch my breath and I felt like I was drowning in a dark sea of depression. I sunk into a whole new world of emptiness and sadness, and I was lower than before. I felt as if I was slipping under the waves and I had nothing to grip onto to stay afloat. Whilst all of this was going on in my head, I continued to portray the façade of being better. I would laugh when I thought I needed to and smiled when I sensed it was appropriate.

The moment soon came when everything I felt inside surfaced and exploded out into the open. Every ounce of strength I used to keep everything bottled up had collapsed from the weight of my depression. My fake smiles eventually fell off my face and the false laughter was silenced. My limit of pretending I was coping was reached and my mask slipped on Mother's Day 2018. All of the emotions I had pushed down during the 'first times,' soon took back the power and had their revenge with me.

I agreed to go shopping for a Mother's Day card and gift with a friend. I felt a twinge of sadness because I couldn't buy something for my own mother, but surprisingly everything else was going well. It wasn't as overwhelming as I had anticipated and I genuinely wasn't battling with the day as I expected to (of course this was all going to change.) As we approached a card shop I started to panic because I saw how many people were inside. I had never been anxious of crowds or large groups before, but I felt sick and my whole body went into a state of rigid numbness. Instead of making an excuse or even just being honest, I stayed quiet and carried on as if everything was ok.

I had no reason to but I resented every person in the shop because they were doing everything I wish I could. These strangers didn't know that of course, and equally I didn't know their situations either. Some people do still buy cards for special occasions for their lost loved ones, but in that moment I didn't care for exceptions. I hated being surrounded by all of these people, who were trying to find the perfect card for their mothers. I felt as if I was an imposter and had no right being there. I felt like I was taking up space in front of the shelves, where people who were actually buying something could be looking. Each second that passed, unwelcomed and overwhelming discussions about people's mothers pierced my ears. The day became more unbearable by the second and the anger inside of me built up just as quick. I can only imagine the sour look I had on my face, because in my head I had already slapped everyone around the face more than twice.

Despite my internal breakdown I found myself picking up cards, scanning over the words and reluctantly placing them back. I was trying to hide from the surrounding noise and each card I looked at I refused to read any of the words. I had become increasingly aware of how awkward my presence was. I wanted to look like I had a reason to be there and not look like the uncomfortable mess I was inside. All of the attempts I tried to distract myself with, from the conversations flying around me fell short. Nothing worked and all I was focused on was everyone's indecisive panic about what card they should get. They were all worrying about the words inside and whether or not their mum would like them. They were criticizing the layouts and the pictures, trying to decide if the card was pretty enough.

All of the constant questions and conversations spun around in my head so fast I felt dizzy. Hearing people bicker about what words sounded more like their mum, and what colour scheme suited their mum better really agitated me. I wanted to scream in the middle of the shop and rip every card up into smithereens. These strangers didn't realise how materialistic and ridiculous they all sounded. They just needed to pick up a stupid card, and write the same message they do each year.

I wanted them to know how it felt to be standing in a card shop; the day before Mother's day listening to people panic about generically written cards when I couldn't buy my mother one. How it felt knowing I couldn't physically watch my mother's facial expression change whilst reading her Mother's day card. I wanted them all to know how it felt that I would never have the opportunity, for the rest of my life to spend another Mother's day with my mother.

Did I say anything? No of course I didn't. Instead I took a deep breath in and continued with the pretence I was fine, but it was harder to fake a smile or fake a laugh. I was so far removed from understanding how happiness felt that I stood cloaked in silence. When my friend was finished getting what she needed, and we had finally walked out of that shop I felt angry. I felt sadness deeper than I had felt before and I felt so lonely. This experience had pushed me further into my dark place and it was on this day where I had truly hit my rock bottom.

Although I do not for a second regret having therapy, I do believe I had it at the wrong time. Therapy helped and it gave me all the support I needed at the time, but if truth be told I hadn't hit my rock bottom back then. When I went to therapy my situation was still so raw and I was obviously sad and low, but I wasn't at the lowest I needed to be. This time around I knew I was in the pit of my rock bottom because, I felt like I did before except it was a thousand times more intense.

I no longer wanted to be around and I had absolutely zero interest in life. I had convinced myself that I had nothing to live for. I was upset every minute of the day and the smallest things would set me off. I wanted to always be alone but I wanted to know someone was around, because I didn't want to be lonely. Everything felt like a contradiction and I was slipping so fast that I didn't have time to understand what was happening. I was standing inside of life with no idea how to live in its concept. The only way I can describe the feeling was like I was standing inside of a tornado and my life was spinning around me.

All I wanted to do was cry all the time and offload my sadness. I needed someone to understand how I was feeling, but how could they when I didn't even understand it (plus I hadn't told anyone how I was feeling.) What I have failed to mention is I had stopped taking my antidepressant medication too (don't worry I didn't go cold turkey.) I had weaned myself off them, decreasing the tablet from a full one to just half daily. I then gradually took one less a day at a time, allowing my body time to adjust and not be left in shock... I had done that by accident once and vowed never again. I forgot to get my repeat prescription and had to wait two weeks and the withdrawal effects were horrendous. For the entire first week, I had electric shock feelings throughout my entire body and I was in a constant state of fear.

However when I started to feel better and convinced myself I was healed, I impulsively decided I no longer needed them at all (correct I made the common mistake!) It was a double edged sword because if I had never stopped taking them, I wouldn't have realised how much I was masking my feelings. I was no longer taking medication and my counselling was finished. I was living in a real life nightmare because I wore a mask around everyone, whilst pretending I wasn't rotting away inside. All the love I once had inside of my heart was haemorrhaging out.

I thought my personality was toxic when I first experienced grief but this time I was poison. Grief was destroying who I was, whoever that person was because I no longer knew. I pushed everyone away because I wanted to be on my own, but I also didn't want anyone to leave me. I was truly in a damaged headspace and I was really scared this time round. I was so desperate for all of this to stop and I feared that one day, I would stop being too afraid to end my life. The suicidal thoughts had now turned into being suicidal but thankfully I was too scared to take action to make it a reality.

I didn't want to end my life despite my mind believing the opposite, I was just unwell and my mental health was unstable. I know that because today I am grateful that I'm still here and I am so thankful I didn't give into my suicidal thoughts. This is why mental health is so scary; you can convince yourself that ending your own life is truly the best thing, not only for yourself but for everyone around you. Now I am not judging or preaching but there is always a way out. Ending your life isn't the only option and it does, and will, affect those around you. People in your life value you and your life even when you don't.

Nobody deserves to feel that ending their life is the only way out. I've seen how suicide rips through a family, we all probably know someone who has been affected by suicide and in no situation, has it ever been for the best. It's hard to fight against the desire to end things and accept that you'll feel like you're nothing for a while. What you need to remember is you're the only person with those thoughts about yourself. I know it isn't that plain and simple but you have to re-programme your mind, your thoughts and your feelings because a temporary moment shouldn't ever be fixed by a permanent solution.

I am sure someone, somewhere needs to hear this and if it's you then read this to yourself out-loud. If it's someone else please read it to them out loud.

You are worthy.

You're worthy of love, worthy of happiness and worthy of life. You're not weak because you're struggling; you're strong because you're surviving. You do not deserve pain, you do not deserve sadness and you have done nothing wrong. You have people who care, who love and who want you around. Your life means the world to someone and without you, their world would collapse. Start living your life because there are people who never had a choice at the end of theirs.

That's what I did... I reminded myself that I felt so lost and devastatingly sad because my mother had lost her life. My mother had her life stripped away from her without choice, and I was thinking about making the choice to strip myself away from life. I couldn't take away the one thing my mother never had a choice to lose. Regardless of how little I thought of it and how rough it felt, I still had the opportunity and the blessing of life. I still had the one thing my mother no longer had and more importantly, this life I believed to be so unworthy, was the last remaining attachment I had to her. My mother gave me this life and I was being ungrateful for it. I am not insinuating that it'll be an easy and effortless experience, because it wasn't for me. It was difficult and at times I still thought *what's the point,* but that's when I fought harder.

I had to fight again and I had to live my life again because I had a choice. I needed a purpose, something to fight for, and towards and I needed a reason to focus on living again. I had to live so that my mother dying wasn't the end for both of us. I believe we have all been born to fulfil a purpose and each one of us have been given the challenge of life, to see what we can do in the time we have.

Chapter Twenty-Three – Finding My Purpose

I really want to make it crystal clear that I never had or found an over-night fix, I took an absolute battering from grief and some days I still do. My whole world collapsed the day I received the call telling me my mum had died. My entire existence and life, how I knew and loved it, was utterly ruined. That day tore a hole in my heart and it will always be there for the rest of my life. No matter how much happiness and joy I have in my heart, I will never fill that missing hole because it represents the missing piece in my life.

My mother's death makes me feel the same excruciating pain today as it did the day it happened. I still hate the reality of not seeing her face, hearing her voice or smelling her perfume. Some days I spray her perfume on me, so I can feel close to her again. I still cry at the loneliness I feel without her here. I cannot put into words or even begin to express how much I miss my mum. There isn't a single second her face, her name or her voice doesn't pass through my mind and that will never change. Every single day is a struggle and I continue to find it hard to accept she's no longer alive. I have never experienced a day that has gotten easier, despite that being the most overused, overpromised, and misleading sentiment said to you after losing someone.

Regardless of how sad I feel or think, I'll always have the power and the choice whether I suffer from it. My journey with grief will never end and I will always grieve my mother for as long as I live. The million dollar question though, is how much do I wish to suffer inside of grief? *Do I want to live inside of grief or do I want grief to live inside of me?* They both have lifelong consequences and they both only have room for one protagonist.

I had to choose between grief being the protagonist, or me being the protagonist of *my* life. I made the decision and I chose me, and I would make the same choice every single time.

I had to fight my way out of the depressive cage I was trapped in again, so I returned to my doctor and asked for a new prescription of Sertraline. I had to go back to medication too, because I couldn't do this unaided. I even got back in contact with my counsellor Dawn, but this was not an aid I would be able to lean on again. The most difficult thing about therapy is the waiting lists. It's a bitter sweet pill really because it shows that people are beginning to speak up and seek the help that they need (which is incredible and everyone who needs help should still reach out,) but it shows the need for more funding to accommodate the growing need.

Unfortunately I would've had to wait three or more months with no guarantee of being seen. At first this terrified me and knocked me a little: just as I was becoming strong again and wanting to fight in the re-match with depression, I was knocked down in the first round. However the important thing was I wasn't knocked out and I was still standing. I may not have the support of therapy this time round, but I'd had it once before and I was given amazing techniques that did work. I was taught how to recognise the triggers, all I needed to do was get back into the habit of practicing it. I already had everything I needed and I could do this without a second round of actual therapy.

I needed a system where I could talk about how I was feeling and that's when I remembered, I had written things down before and how much it helped me. I found the file I had saved on my laptop and began re-reading what I had written. That's when I acknowledged how much I had neglected my emotions and feelings. Everything I read was exactly how I was feeling again, only it was a whole world more aggressive. *This is exactly how I will record my emotions and feelings.* It was perfect… I had my own therapist, and it was me, myself and I. I had somewhere to talk freely and not feel ashamed, I had an outlet… I had me.

I would pick up my laptop and spend a whole day just writing until it became my routine, and that's when I decided to write a book. I decided to turn all of my emotions, all of my feelings and my heartbreak into a book. What first started out as a journal for my thoughts, manifested itself into an ambition, a focus and what I now consider to be my purpose. I had found my purpose in the wreckage I was surrounded by, and for the first time I truly saw the way out of my darkness. I had something to grip onto and use as the rope to pull myself back into life again.

Did I know what I was doing?

Did I know how I was going to turn my journal into a book?

Did I really understand how hard it would be?

I had without question, no idea what I was doing. I didn't have the first idea how to transform what I was feeling into a book. More importantly I had absolutely and categorically no bloody idea how hard this would be. There have been countless times I wanted to stop, to give up and forget about it. I've asked myself on numerous occasions: *what's the point? Why am I even doing this?* The answer is simple: the reason I never gave up was because we spend so much time focusing on the end results, and become so fixated on the bigger picture, that we neglect the present and the moment.

I forgot to do that and I enabled myself to drop back into the deep end of depression because I took my eye off the ball. I stopped focusing on what was happening in the moment and instead, I was more concerned on being better, being fixed and all of the long term aims. I didn't stand a chance of getting better or healing when I didn't focus on the journey of actually getting there first. So I stopped asking myself these questions and I focused on the present. I was writing what I needed to write and I wrote when I needed to write, nothing more and nothing less.

It wasn't just writing that helped me, I decided to give myself a break too. If I felt sad one day, I allowed myself to feel it but I remembered what made me sad. I was using every day as a lesson to teach me how I can make sure every other day was better. If I felt happy one day, I'd evaluate what made me happy and why, then I'd make sure I did more of that every other day. I took the pressure off myself and I didn't guilt myself into getting or feeling better. I allowed myself time, I spent more time learning about myself than teaching myself. After all, I was a different person to who I once was. Things that once made me tick and made me smile no longer worked. I needed to learn what did and I had to connect to the person I had become, because I didn't know her. How could I possibly know what would make her heal, if I didn't know what made her happy?

Little by little I started to get to know myself again and I began to understand who I was. I recognised when, what and who made me feel happy. I spent less time focusing on the 'if's' and more time on the 'when's,' and I naturally became more and more positive each day that passed. It doesn't matter if something bad happens it matters how you deal with it. We will all have bad days, it's a given, but how we handle those days and what can we gain from them is what counts. It really doesn't have to always be bleak, there is nothing wrong, hippy or weird about being positive. You can still live in a realistic world and be positive.

It's not about being happy 24/7 because that's impossible, it's having a really shit day, week or month (who else just sung the F.R.I.E.N.D.S theme tune,) but knowing and wanting to have better times after. That's reality and that is life, you can have good and bad in the same week and in the same day even, but recognising not every day will be like is what being positive is.

I had a new focus in my life and a creative outlet which lit a fire within me. I had created a space for myself, somewhere I could go to face up to my demons, and it allowed me to accept the death of my mother and finally begin to heal properly. In order for me to write this book, I've had to relive specific moments in my life, and they made me feel emotions I thought were gone. I've had to replay moments of my journey that I never wanted to think about again. Yet doing this I've addressed my grief and I have given myself the time and space to accept that my mother is no longer alive. Through reliving my trauma instead of blocking it out and pretending it doesn't exist, I have started to heal.

There have been days and nights I've sobbed my heart out and the hardest chapter to write and relive was the day mum died. Things came back to me about that day I didn't even realise had happened, and that ripped my heart into shreds. I didn't think it was possible to feel the same heartbreak twice but I did. I remember half way through writing that chapter; I had to stop because I was sobbing uncontrollably and couldn't see my screen. I thought that was where I would draw the line and stop writing it altogether. I had no idea how I would get through it (once again completely focusing on the end result,) failing to recognise that I needed to do it so I could accept it had happened.

Here's a really cheesy story about that chapter actually, I used to think people were lying when they used to say things like this…

I was sat in my living room on my own, (thankfully) when I had to stop half way through that chapter because I couldn't see my screen, I closed my eyes trying to stop my cries. As I opened them I looked at the picture of mum hanging on the wall, and asked for her to help because I couldn't do this without her. I felt like a right idiot to be honest, but I tried to shake it off by making a cup of tea. After I was done I came back in and got comfy again, before I started again I put my music on (I created a writing playlist,) and the first song that came on was: Demi Lovato – Tell me you love me.

I didn't start writing again, instead I just sat and listened to the song. When the chorus hit I felt something change within me. As the lyrics changed to: *oh tell me you love me, I need someone on days like this, I do, on days like this, oh can you hear my heart say?* I felt a fire ignite inside me, and I had so much determination to finish the chapter. I had that song on repeat, every day until it was finished. Now before any of this happened to me I would have said: *So what? You heard a song and you started writing again, what's the big deal?* The person I am today though see's everything differently, I believe I was meant to hear that song, in that moment and on that day. I am a strong believer in the law of attraction and getting back what you put out. I asked for mum's help and this was her way of telling me to keep going. It was her way of showing me she was watching and she was around.

I am so much more connected to spirituality now and I have become conscious to the energies around me. I feel completely suppressed around negative energy (it's the strangest feeling.) I think we become more aware of the energies around us, when we are aware and connected to ourselves. Some people may think this is a load of tripe so I won't preach about crystals, or recommend the best place to buy Palo Santo sticks. What I will say is spirituality came to me once I was completely content and aware of myself. I know and understand what makes me feel at my best and what doesn't. We all have the ability to do it and all you need to do is lose the outside pressures and connect with your authentic self.

I was set free when I connected with who I am, what genuinely makes me happy and what actually upsets me. I believe there is nothing in this world that can make you happy until you're happy within first.

There is no sum of money, no flash possessions, no status and certainly no one else that can create happiness for you, they can only add to or suppress it. The only thing or person in control of creating it is you, but if you don't know who you are, how will you ever really know what truly makes you happy?

The journey of writing this book has been so important to me, because we all deserve to be happy and content in the life we live. Mental health is a seriously taboo subject, and people still struggle to grasp the concept that, a person can be unwell even if they don't show physical signs.

People still use harmful and hurtful references to describe mental health conditions and the people living with them. I would like to believe that the only reason people still use a stereotype is due to of a lack of education. I can't accept that if people really understood what it's like to live with depression, anxiety or any other condition that they would still be so vulgar. I also want to believe stigmas are only attached out of fear and not people being able to relate.

I hope that in my life time I get to see appropriate, specialised and researched mental health treatment. No one deserves to feel like they are not normal and like they're less than anyone else. Everyone should feel safe, healthy and worthy in this world. Each and every single one of us has mental health. None of us are immune to ill health of any kind... So please, the next time you walk past someone who doesn't look like they're ok, don't walk past and judge. Stop and ask them because you'll never know, one day that could be you and I promise you, you'll never feel so alone in all of your life. For anybody who is currently experiencing ill mental health, I promise you there is always a choice. You do not have to suffer; you have the choice to either be powered by your mental health, or to have the power over your mental health. Don't choose to give up because you've already got this far to stop fighting. You need to know that you're worthy of happiness and life. Please don't be afraid to reach out for help, it doesn't mean you are weak, or a failure and you are not crazy.

You are not defined by your mental health, it does not represent who you are and it does not own you. Your mental health lives inside of you, not the other way around. You own your body and you own your mind so you control what happens to it. You are normal and you're always going to be normal, the only thing that ever changes is your normality. You will always be you so learn to accept it, learn to appreciate it and more importantly, learn to love it. Learn what your purpose is.

I found my purpose in writing and it gave me back the enjoyment to life. Finding my purpose came when I decided to accept my new normality, and after I decided to accept I was normal. Everything I went through was normal because after all, I was grieving the death of my mother.

Unfortunately I had to lose a piece of my world to gain the purpose for my life.

My purpose was to share my journey in the hopes it helps others. My purpose was to honour my mother and I can't explain how fulfilling it is, I just wish she was here to share it with me. So my final words to survive this world are simple: Find your purpose, work for it, work at it and don't stop until you become it.

Printed in Great Britain
by Amazon

71147479R00241